大学实用英语写作教程

（第3版）

PRACTICAL ENGLISH WRITING FOR COLLEGE STUDENTS (3RD EDITION)

主编◎刘 宁　张莱湘　汪 宏
编者◎王 红　郭 瑞　沈莉霞　吴业军　许子艳
　　　闫丽华　王 宁　罗 勤　毕晓宁
主审◎David Parkinson

北京理工大学出版社
BEIJING INSTITUTE OF TECHNOLOGY PRESS

版权专有　侵权必究

图书在版编目（CIP）数据

大学实用英语写作教程/刘宁，张莱湘，汪宏主编．—3 版．—北京：北京理工大学出版社，2015.8（2023.1 重印）

ISBN 978-7-5682-1132-1

Ⅰ．①大…　Ⅱ．①刘…　②张…　③汪…　Ⅲ．①英语-写作-高等学校-教材　Ⅳ．①H315

中国版本图书馆 CIP 数据核字（2015）第 199995 号

出版发行 / 北京理工大学出版社有限责任公司
社　　址 / 北京市海淀区中关村南大街 5 号
邮　　编 / 100081
电　　话 /（010）68914775（总编室）
　　　　　（010）82562903（教材售后服务热线）
　　　　　（010）68944723（其他图书服务热线）
网　　址 / http：//www.bitpress.com.cn
经　　销 / 全国各地新华书店
印　　刷 / 北京虎彩文化传播有限公司
开　　本 / 787 毫米×1092 毫米　1/16
印　　张 / 12.75　　　　　　　　　　　　　　　责任编辑 / 梁铜华
字　　数 / 250 千字　　　　　　　　　　　　　　文案编辑 / 梁铜华
版　　次 / 2015 年 8 月第 3 版　2023 年 1 月第 4 次印刷　责任校对 / 周瑞红
定　　价 / 38.00 元　　　　　　　　　　　　　　责任印制 / 王美丽

图书出现印装质量问题，请拨打售后服务热线，本社负责调换

Purpose of Writing

People write for many reasons and to achieve many goals. Some write for themselves (in diaries and memos), while others write for thousands (magazine, newspaper, speech and novel writers). Undoubtedly, it is a specific way of communication and comprehension. People write to entertain, to inform, to explain, to argue, to support, to judge and to persuade others to do or think about a subject in a different way. In all cases, people have to write clearly and effectively in order to express exactly their inner minds, their deep feelings or their careful thoughts, even their insight into and their observation on the outer world.

Introduction to Standard English Writing

When it comes to a good English writing, or rather a standard English writing, first of all, the learners are supposed to answer the following open question: Is there a standard English? Many people would argue that there is not a "standard" English. Take American English and British English as an example. People can hardly tell which of them is not standard, let alone Australian English, Singapore English and many other varieties of English. Then, is there a "standard" English writing? Suppose the answer to this question is "YES" (because anyone who writes should obey the rules of English writing, such as the spelling, grammar and sentence structure), then, who is the judge to identify the standard and what is the measure to achieve it?

- **Rationale**

To ensure that the writing is understood and well-received, writers need a working knowledge of language as well as grammatical structures, diction and usage, punctuation, spelling, layout and presentation. Such knowledge is also invaluable for discussing, revising and editing written communication in any form.

- **Reader's view**

It is widely accepted that the purpose of writing is to exchange ideas and thoughts, even to argue with the targeted audience. In this sense, in writing, reader's view has become the concern of the writer. Generally speaking, readers feel pleasant and comfortable when the written work has the following features, or when it is:

— **clear** in both the intended thesis and the controlling ideas;

— **concise** in the language and structures;

— **comprehensible** to the reader; and

— **recognizable**, which mainly refers to the clear handwriting.

In short, a well-written work is always a benefit to the reader.

Requirement of Standard English

In all cases, however, the criterion of a "standard" English writing definitely differs from that of writing "standard" English. The former concerns about the audience's response, while the latter depends on the writer's ability to use the correct spelling, punctuation and grammar that helps him/her communicate easily. Writers are also expected to meet the following demands in their writing:

— some well-thought-out, critical questions on the essay;

— a clear introduction of the writing to the reader;

— a clear, coherent and logical writing style;

— a range of supporting evidence; and

— a conclusion.

Basic Principles of English Writing

Apart from the intellectual abilities of the writer, such as the ability to criticize, conceptual skills, and abilities to initiate and select organizational materials, and the skills in using correct grammar and proper vocabulary, writers should take the following into account:

— be aware of the writing assignment or situation and start by playing with ideas;

— focus on ideas and be specific;

— select details that fit the focus and keep it clear;

— write the ending; and

— rethink, reorganize, rewrite.

To sum up, the writing ability, among many other language skills, is well acquired through targeted teaching and everyday practice.

> **Tell me, I will forget;**
> **Show me, I may remember;**
> **Involve me, I will understand.**

Contents

PART ONE THE ESSENTIAL GUIDE TO ENGLISH WRITING

Chapter One Basic Principles of English Writing ···002
- 1.1 Basic Skills of English Writing ···002
- 1.2 Spoken English vs. Written English ···003
- 1.3 Punctuation ···004
- 1.4 Mechanics ···010
- 1.5 Procedure of Writing ···016
- 1.6 Words ···020
- 1.7 Sentences ···022

Chapter Two Paragraph Writing ···029
- 2.1 Paragraph Structure ···029
- 2.2 Ways to Enhance Coherence ···031

PART TWO COMPOSING ESSAYS

Chapter Three Narration ···043
- 3.1 Employment of Various Points of View ···043
- 3.2 Thesis Statement ···045
- 3.3 Organization ···047
- 3.4 Supporting Details ···048

Chapter Four Description ···052

Chapter Five Exposition ···055
- 5.1 Expository Essay of Definition ···056
- 5.2 Expository Essay of Process ···059

- 5.3 Expository Essay of Classification/Division ... 059
- 5.4 Expository Essay of Cause-and-effect ... 062
- 5.5 Expository Essay of Problem-and-solution ... 064
- 5.6 Expository Essay of Comparison and Contrast ... 066
- 5.7 Expository Essay of Exemplification ... 069
- 5.8 Expository Essay of Listing ... 070

Chapter Six Argumentation ... 077
- 6.1 Argumentative Essay—Pattern 1 ... 079
- 6.2 Argumentative Essay—Pattern 2 ... 080
- 6.3 Argumentative Essay—Pattern 3 ... 082
- 6.4 Argumentative Essay—Pattern 4 ... 084
- 6.5 More Samples of Argumentative Essays ... 084

Chapter Seven Illustration Description ... 089
- 7.1 Figure and Chart Description ... 089
- 7.2 Cartoon Description ... 103

PART THREE WRITING FOR PRACTICAL PURPOSES

Chapter Eight Personal Letters and Social Correspondences ... 112
- 8.1 Format and Envelope of a Letter ... 112
- 8.2 Invitation Letter ... 119
- 8.3 Thank-you Letter ... 122
- 8.4 Letter of Condolence and Consolation ... 124
- 8.5 Letter of Congratulations ... 128

Chapter Nine Applying for University Admission ... 131
- 9.1 Requesting for an Admission Form ... 131
- 9.2 Graduation Certification and Notarization ... 133
- 9.3 Personal Statement ... 134
- 9.4 Letter of Recommendation ... 138

Chapter Ten Employment Writing ... 141
- 10.1 Cover Letter ... 141
- 10.2 Résumé ... 143
- 10.3 Curriculum Vitae ... 147

Chapter Eleven Note and Memo 151

Chapter Twelve Notice and Poster 155

PART FOUR ACADEMIC WRITING

Chapter Thirteen Summary Writing 159
    13.1 Steps in Writing a Summary 159
    13.2 The Checklist for Organizing a Summary 160

Chapter Fourteen Abstract Writing 169
    14.1 What Is an Abstract? 169
    14.2 Some Conventions of Abstract Writing 169
    14.3 Different Types of Abstract 170
    14.4 The Formalized Structure of Abstract 170

Chapter Fifteen Writing for Delivery 176
    15.1 Report 176
    15.2 Proposal 180
    15.3 Seminar 181
    15.4 Presentation 183
    15.5 Viva 183
    15.6 Public Speech 184

Suggested Answers 187

PART ONE
THE ESSENTIAL GUIDE TO ENGLISH WRITING

Introduction

The objective of writing is to express the ideas concisely and clearly to readers so that communication is achieved as quickly and accurately as possible. To this end, two elements are fundamental in writing: **language** and **content**, i.e. good language and clear ideas.

These two elements together can generate good writing. However, if we have nothing worth writing, even the best writing skills cannot help. Similarly, if we have good ideas but cannot express them well in writing, the reader will not benefit. A good writing should not be a guessing game for the reader or an exercise in error correction for the teacher.

PART ONE of this textbook introduces the basic elements of a good English writing, including basic skills of English writing and the writing process, such as the use of right punctuation, proper word choice, effective sentence structure, as well as some necessary training on the targeted techniques.

Chapter One

Basic Principles of English Writing

1.1 Basic Skills of English Writing

1.1.1 A pre-test

Before we begin discussing about the principles of English writing, learners are expected to be aware that some ideas about writing are not true. Please read the following statements carefully and tell if they are **True** or **False**.

(1) You need to be inspired to write.

(2) You have to have a "real gift" for writing.

(3) If you write a good first sentence, then all the other sentences will flow out.

(4) All you have to do is to follow a step-by-step procedure, including making an outline.

(5) You should try to impress your readers with your large vocabulary.

(All the above statements are false or partly true.)

1.1.2 Basic principles of writing

Prior to writing, there are usually some questions the writer will confront. For example, some assignments may appear to be either too general or too narrow. Consequently, learners will have to figure out what to do and how to do it. In either case, remind yourself of the following steps.

(1) Think about the writing assignment or situation.

(2) Get started by playing with ideas.

(3) Be specific.

(4) Focus your ideas.

(5) Select details that fit the focus.

(6) Keep the focus clear.

(7) Connect related parts.

(8) Write an ending.

(9) Rethink, reorganize, rewrite.

1.2 Spoken English vs. Written English

Spoken English refers to the English spoken in our ordinary everyday life. **Written English** refers to a formal kind of English that is commonly used in academic and scientific books. Whether to tell a story or write it down, we need to take at least five elements into consideration: the content, the structure, the context, the audience/readers and the feedback. That is to say, whether to speak well or to write well, we need to have good and well-organized ideas and present them in the right context. In addition, we ought to know about the audience, their interests and their needs. As to writing, we have to arrange it in a logical way for the target readers and make efforts to identify it with their needs so as to involve their identification likewise.

Although both spoken and written English are communication activities sharing many common characteristics in content, structure, context, audience, feedback, etc., it is evident that they differ from each other in many aspects. These differences mainly fall into two categories: the choice of words and the way these words are put together to form sentences.

1.2.1 The choice of words

According to a survey from Cambridge University in 1997, the 50 most frequent words out of the 330,000 words of Cambridge International Corpus are as follows:

No.	W	S	No.	W	S	No.	W	S	No.	W	S	No.	W	S
1	the	the	11	it	in	21	be	they	31	are	for	41	their	don't
2	to	I	12	on	was	22	my	well	32	an	this	42	she	she
3	of	you	13	he	is	23	have	what	33	this	just	43	who	think
4	a	and	14	is	it's	24	from	yes	34	has	all	44	if	if
5	and	to	15	with	know	25	had	have	35	been	there	45	him	with
6	in	it	16	you	no	26	by	we	36	up	like	46	we	then
7	I	a	17	but	oh	27	me	he	37	were	one	47	about	at
8	was	yeah	18	at	so	28	her	do	38	out	be	48	will	about
9	for	that	19	his	but	29	they	got	39	when	right	49	all	are
10	that	of	20	as	on	30	not	that's	40	one	not	50	would	as
Note: W=written; S=spoken														

It is obvious that in Spoken English, people prefer to choose the easy and simple words with some slangs and vogue words being used sometimes. On the contrary, in Written English, the choice of vocabulary is more academic and professional:

Spoken English vs. Written English

Spoken English	Written English
get, *win*	*acquire, obtain, procure, receive*
give	*accord, award, confer, donate, equip, provide, supply*
make	*fabricate, manufacture, produce*

1.2.2 Sentence structure

Spoken English and Written English use different sentence structures. Sentences in Spoken English are usually shorter with repetitions, incomplete sentences, correction and interruptions, because they are usually used for immediate interactions. On the other hand, Written English tends to be more complex and intricate with longer sentences and many subordinate clauses. In addition, standard grammar and rhetoric features are also frequently used in writing.

Ex. 1-2-1 *Rewrite the following sentences with Spoken English.*

1. At the counter, we inquired about the arrival time of the aircraft.
2. He eradicated all the imperfections in his notes.
3. She contemplated his utterance.
4. Paul was terminated from his employment.
5. Personnel are requested to extinguish illumination before departure from these premises.
6. Unfortunately, we are not in a position to offer assistance to you.
7. Our university is in close proximity to an amusement park.
8. Terry is of the opinion that everything will be going on smoothly.

1.3 Punctuation

Punctuation refers to the use of standard marks and signs in writing to divide a piece of writing into sentences, clauses and phrases so as to clarify the meaning.

For example, the following two sentences with the same words but different punctuation marks carry different meanings.

c.f.

Woman, without her man, is nothing.
Woman, without her, man is nothing.

Proper use of punctuation is of great importance, for it can change the meanings of sentences completely. As a device to help us read and understand a piece of writing, correct punctuation mark is an efficient assistant to both the completeness of language and the accuracy of contents.

The principal punctuation marks and their names are as follows:

(1) Period/full stop: [.].
(2) Comma: [,].
(3) Hyphen: [-].
(4) Apostrophe: ['].
(5) Semicolon: [;].
(6) Colon: [:].
(7) Question mark: [?].
(8) Quotation marks: [" "].
(9) Exclamation mark : [!].
(10) Dash: [–].
(11) Brackets: : [( ), [ ], < >, { }].
(12) Ellipsis: […].
(13) Asterisk: [*].
(14) Pound: [#].
(15) At: [@].

The use of punctuation marks in English shares great similarities with those in Chinese. However, there are also some differences. For example:

(1) Period/full stop in English: [.]; in Chinese: [。].
(2) Ellipsis in English: […]; in Chinese: [……].
(3) There is no [、] in English. We use [,] in English to separate the words, clauses and sentences, while in Chinese we use [、] instead.
(4) In Chinese, [《 》] is employed to quote the title of a book, a paper, a magazine, etc. However, the quotation marks [" "] are preferable to modify the titles of passages and songs, while the titles of books or other longer works, when printed, are usually italicized.
(5) The dash in English is made up of two hyphens [–], leaving no space before, between or after them, while in Chinese it is a bit longer.

1. Period/full stop

Period/full stop is used:

1) At the end of a statement, a mild command or an indirect question.

   e.g.

   Mary is a lovely girl.

Please pass me the salt.

I am wondering what is going on.

2) To indicate an abbreviation.

e.g.

Mr. Smith; the U. S. A.

A period/full stop is not used in abbreviations of names or organizations and government agencies (such as NBC: National Broadcasting Corporation). When the abbreviation comes at the end of a sentence, one period is adequate while in the middle of a sentence, an abbreviation often has a period/full stop followed by a comma (.,).

e.g.

In 1987, he lived in the U.S.A.

While he was living in the U.S.A., he worked as a taxi driver.

2. Comma

Comma is used between two complete sentences, joined together by **and, but, or, for, nor, so, yet**, etc. It is applied:

1) To separate items in a series or list, but it is normally not used between the last two items.

e.g.

There are many fruits on the table: apples, pears, grapes and pineapples.

2) Before **and, but, or, nor, for, yet** and *so* when the word joins two coordinate clauses.

e.g.

I have to come back earlier, for it is my mother's birthday.

3) To mark off sentences or clauses where a pause is needed in reading.

e.g.

Jones, come with me.

4) To separate adjectives which describe the same noun.

e.g.

a tall, dark and handsome young man

5) To mark off participial elements, when a pause is required in reading.

e.g.

Tom is lying in bed, reading a novel.

6) To mark off short words and phrases, such as **yes, no, well, oh, nevertheless, after all, at last, all in all,** etc.

e.g.

Yes, I am a sophomore in Beijing Institute of Technology.

7) Before **too** when it means **also**.

e.g.

Nice to meet you, too.

8) To separate words that might confuse the reader if they are read together.

e.g.

Before, the party cheered us up.

*Before the party cheered us up.

> **Note:**
> * refers to unacceptable usage

Tips:

- No comma before *"that"* when it is used to lead a subordinate clause, nor when the word or phrase gives necessary information.

    e.g.

    The box that was on the shell has disappeared.

    Their daughter Susan just graduated from high school.

- Sometimes, pairs of commas [, ,] are used:

    ① To mark off parenthetical words or phrases like **however, therefore, of course, for instance**, etc.

    e.g.

    The book, however, is worth it though it's expensive.

    ② To set off an appositive.

    e.g.

    Jane, my sister, is a nurse.

    ③ To set off non-restrictive clauses.

    e.g.

    Tom, who lives next-door, hasn't arrived yet.

3. Hyphen

Hyphen is used:

1) To make compound words.

    e.g.

    well-dressed; bad-tempered

2) To spell out a number between twenty and one hundred.

    e.g.

    fifty-five

3) To join the two parts of a word when it runs out of room at the end of a line.

4. Apostrophe

Apostrophe is used:

1) To indicate possession (The general rule is to add an apostrophe and "s" to the word required).

   e.g.

   Mary's father; Jack's book

2) To indicate the omission of letters in contracted forms.

   e.g.

   can't; it's; aren't

3) When the first two figures of the number of a year are left out.

   e.g.

   An incident occurred in '82.

> **Note:**
> If there is already an "s" at the end of a word, do not add a second one, unless the word is singular, *e.g. wives'; ladies'.*

5. Semicolon

A semicolon is stronger than a comma and weaker than a period/full stop and it connects only equal ranks, but too strong to be used often.

e.g.

He had in his hand, a pistol; in his boot, a knife; in his belt, a sword; in his eyes, a gleam of hatred.

It is usually used:

1) Between independent clauses not joined by coordinating conjunctions **(and, but, or, nor, so, yet,** etc.).

   e.g.

   His wife won't let him; she is afraid he might get hurt.

2) With words like **therefore, however, nevertheless, otherwise, besides, also** and sometimes **so**. These words are sometimes used to join sentences. As they are stronger than conjunctions **like**, they need a stronger punctuation mark.

   e.g.

   The new machine is in urgent need; therefore, we have two work shifts to meet the demand.

6. Colon

A colon introduces an explanation or an example. It is used:

1) To show that the following is a fuller explanation of what has been stated.

   e.g.

This book is quite interesting: it contains many popular fairy tales for the children.

2) To introduce a list of items, especially when the list comes after words "***as follows***" or "***the following***."

e.g.

All campers must bring the following things: matches, a tent and a flashlight.

3) To introduce quotations.

e.g.

Jack shouted loudly: "Who is there?"

7. Quotation mark

1) Quotation marks are used to enclose direct speech.

e.g.

"You are right," the teacher smiled.

2) **Single quotation marks** are applied to enclose a direct quotation within a quotation.

e.g.

"How to spell the word 'quotation', please?"

8. Question mark

A question mark is used after any kind of direct question, including requests beginning with "***Will you …?***" etc. and after expressions like "***isn't it?***."

e.g.

Will you go swimming with us tomorrow?

It's a nice day, isn't it?

9. Exclamation mark

The exclamation mark suggests surprise, enthusiasm or loud speech, especially after exclamations like "***Oh!,***" "***Hello!,***" etc. and after exclamatory sentences without a main verb as "***Good job!***," "***What a nice day!***," "***How beautiful!***."

10. Dash

A dash is used to emphasize that the thought is interrupted or unfinished.

e.g.

She replied: "I will be back in two days—I mean, in three days."

11. Brackets

Brackets are used for words that give explanatory but not absolutely essential information.

e.g.

His sister (a student in Beijing Institute of Technology) is the excellent graduate this year.

12. Ellipsis

An ellipsis may indicate the omission of certain words or a long pause, during which the reader may be directed to think about what has been said and draw his own conclusions.

e.g.

We hold these truths to be self-evident: that all men ... are endowed by their Creator with certain unalienable rights.

Ex. 1-3-1 *Read the following sentences, and put the correct punctuation marks in the right places. Add CAPITAL LETTERS where necessary.*

1. Come early or youll be late for school
2. It must be raining now for everyone carries an umbrella
3. The engineer who is talking there is Jack's father
4. Do you believe in the saying that blood is thicker than water
5. The director in fact has done very little work
6. The Temple of Heaven he said is like a fairyland
7. She was born on Aug 5 1996
8. I mean well I mean we neednt come back so early
9. No one is born with knowledge knowledge must be taught and learned
10. Christopher G Hayes wrote a very useful book for students English at Hand 2003
11. The drowning girl was screaming help help
12. On the fourth of july we celebrate the war of independence on labor day we celebrate the contributions of organized labor to American life
13. As a salesperson he lives by this motto never sell a product I myself have never used and like.
14. Poor management insufficient supplies of raw material and shortage of skilled workers these are the main reason for the failure of this enterprise.

1.4　Mechanics

Mechanics in this section is referred to as the instructions on format, capital words, italics, numbers as well as abbreviations.

1.4.1　Format

Follow the instructions after the model when preparing a writing task. It is for both handwritten and computer-written work.

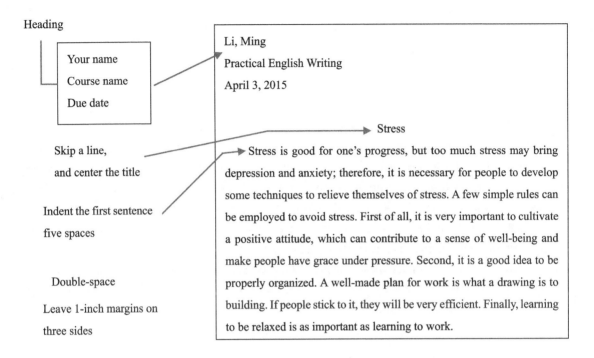

Note:

1. **Paper:** Use 8 $^{1/2}$-inch-by-11-inch, *i.e.* A4 white paper.

2. **Font:** Use a standard font, such as Times New Roman. **Don't use underlining, italics or bold type to emphasize words**. It is not correct to do so in academic writing because they are used only when required for titles of books and some other publications.

3. **Heading:** Type your full name in the upper left corner 1/2 inch from the top of the page. On the next line, type the course name or number. On the third line of the heading, type the date the assignment is due in the order month-day-year with a comma after the day.

4. **Assignment Title:** Skip one line, and then center your title. Use the centering icon on your word processing program.

5. **Body:** Skip one line and use the TAB key to indent (move to the right) the first line of the paragraph.

6. **Margins:** Leave a 1-inch margin on the left and right.

7. **Spacing:** Double-space the body.

For the writing of an essay with several paragraphs, two options of format are available for writers: block and indented.

Indented Format

Li, Ming
Practical English Writing
April 3, 2015

Stress

  We all suffer from stress in our lives. Some people are afraid of stress and consider it to be negative while others find it a positive factor for personal development. In their opinion, the more stress they have, the bigger the challenges they will meet and the more achievements they will make.

  Stress is good for one's progress, but too much stress may bring depression and anxiety; therefore, it is necessary for people to develop some techniques to relieve themselves of stress. A few simple rules can be employed to avoid stress. First of all, it is very important to cultivate a positive attitude, which can contribute to a sense of well-being and make people have grace under pressure. Second, it is a good idea to be properly organized. A well-made plan for work is what a drawing is to building. If people stick to it, they will be very efficient. Finally, learning to be relaxed is as important as learning to work.

  To sum up, stress is common and the key is knowing how to cope with it.

Block Format

Li, Ming
Practical English Writing
April 3, 2015

Stress

We all suffer from stress in our lives. Some people are afraid of stress and consider it to be negative while others find it a positive factor for personal development. In their opinion, the more stress they have, the bigger the challenges they will meet and the more achievements they will make.

Stress is good for one's progress, but too much stress may bring depression and anxiety; therefore, it is necessary for people to develop some techniques to relieve themselves of stress. A few simple rules can be employed to avoid stress. First of all, it is very important to cultivate a positive attitude, which can contribute to a sense of well-being and make people have grace under pressure. Second, it is a good idea to be properly organized. A well-made plan for work is what a drawing is to building. If people stick to it, they will be very efficient. Finally, learning to be relaxed is as important as learning to work.

To sum up, stress is common and the key is knowing how to cope with it.

1.4.2 Capitalization

The rules of capitalization are rather extensive and depend somewhat on the context in which the words are used. When we are writing a composition, capitalize the following:

(1) The first letter of the first word in a sentence or direct quotation.

e.g.

*The ice-cream man said, "**T**ry a frozen banana bar. **T**hey are so delicious."*

(2) The word "***I***" and interjection "***O***".

e.g.

*How, **O** ye gods, can **I** control this joy?*

(3) The first word of an independent clause that follows a colon. (When an independent clause comes after a colon, capitalize when what follows the colon is a question, a lengthy statement or a point to emphasize.)

e.g.

*There is one thing that all people who accomplish a lot do: **T**hey organize their time.*

(4) The titles. [Capitalize the first, last and important words in the title of a book, magazine, newspaper, article, paper, play, film, television program, song, poem or story. Articles (a, an, the), short prepositions and short conjunctions are not capitalized unless they begin or end a title. However, a preposition or a conjunction of five or more letters is usually capitalized.]

e.g.

*The title of my paper is **A** **C**omparison and **C**ontrast **B**etween **H**amlet and **D**eath of a **S**alesman.*

(5) Opening and closing a letter. (Capitalize all the words in the salutation of a letter. Capitalize only the first word of the closing of a letter.)

e.g.

***D**ear **M**s. **J**ohnson; **D**ear **S**ir or **M**adam*

***S**incerely yours; **Y**ours truly*

(6) Abbreviations.

e.g.

NBA; NASA; IBM

(7) Proper nouns and adjectives. (Capitalize the first letters of proper names, the essential words of proper names formed with common words and words made from proper nouns but not general terms.)

e.g.

***A**frica; **W**orld **W**ar **II**; **N**ational **D**ay; **E**nglish; **A**unt **M**ary; **D**r. **S**mith; **B**ible; **Y**oung **P**ioneer*

1.4.3 Italics

Italics is often indicated by underlining in handwriting and typing, while in print, slanting is always adopted instead.

Italics is used:

(1) For titles of books, magazines, newspapers, motion pictures, musical compositions, plays and other works of arts.

e.g.

We have to finish reading the book *Great Expectations* this week.

(2) For names of ships, trains and airplanes.

e.g.

Colombia, *Discovery* and *Atlantis* are famous American space shuttles.

(3) For foreign words in the context of an English sentence.

e.g.

The electronic dictionary can translate the English words into Chinese and *vice versa*.

Tips:

Some words borrowed from other languages have already become a part of English language and therefore should not be italicized.

e.g.

disco (French); pizza (Italian); dilemma (Greek)

---

(4) For words, letters or figures being named or emphasized.

e.g.

The letter *k* in *knight* is not pronounced.

1.4.4 Numbers

Numbers are used in writing in the following ways:

(1) Spell out any number that can be written in one or two words; otherwise, use numerals.

e.g.

When I turned **twenty-two**, I went on a ***fifteen***-day trip across the south of China.

(2) Spell out any number that begins a sentence.

e.g.

Eight hundred and sixty-one dollars was found in this wallet.

(3) Use numerals to show time, dates, address, decimals, percentages, page numbers and divisions of a book.

e.g.

*7 a.m. (but seven o'clock); July **2, 2015;** 5 South Zhongguancun Street; **78%;** Part **6***

1.4.5 Abbreviation

In general, most abbreviations should be avoided in formal writing. However, they are appropriate in the following situations:

(1) Titles used before and after people's names.

e.g.

Dr. *Smith;* **St.** *Thomas*

(2) Initials in a person's name.

e.g.

*Dahnne **A.** Miller; **T.** Martin Sawyer*

(3) Specific time and date references.

e.g.

*The lecture will begin at 4:45 **p.m**.*

*Muslin calculate their calendar from Friday, July 16, **A.D.** 622.*

(4) Organizations, agencies, countries and corporations known by their initials and acronyms.

e.g.

USA; NBC; FBI; AIDS

Tips:

In formal writing, do not abbreviate the following:

(1) **Personal name.**

e.g.

*****Geo.** Washington's first inauguration was made in 1789.

George Washington's first inauguration was made in 1789.

(2) **States and countries.**

e.g.

*The company's headquarters are in **Mpls., Minn**.

The company's headquarters are in **Minneapolis, Minnesota**.

(3) **Days of the week and months.**

e.g.

*We are moving out on the first **Mon.** in **Dec.**

We are moving out on the first **Monday** in **December**.

(4) **Holidays.**

e.g.

> *We are planning to go back home for **Xmas**.
>
> We are planning to go back home for **Christmas**.
>
> (5) **School courses.**
>
> e.g.
>
> *I select the course **Ab. Psych.** this semester.
>
> I select the course **Abnormal Psychology** this semester.

Ex. 1-4-1 *Correct the mistakes in the following sentences.*

1. The reply is always "not today."

2. On sun., 10/10, we spent the night in Oklahoma; The next day we flew to south America.

3. While waiting for the dentist, i read an article on "American Politics" in an old issue of U.S. News & World Report.

4. My dog is 8 years old—that's 56 in people years.

5. I like the good old days when Lincoln's birthday always fell on Feb. Twelfth.

6. Spelling errors involving the substitution of d for t in such words as partner and pretty reflect a tendency in pronunciation.

7. Tina now has one thousand one hundred and forty-five records in her collection.

8. I will have the first appt. with My eye dr., Dr. C. I. Glass early next mon.

9. For letter writing, you can refer to the Random house handbook.

10. My courses in this semester include English Grammar, American history, general psychology and computer operation.

1.5 Procedure of Writing

1.5.1 Word choice

Compare the words in the columns below:

begin	commence establish initiate institute instigate originate	give	accord award confer donate equip provide supply

It is obvious that written English has a much larger vocabulary than spoken English. Generally speaking, in spoken English the words are usually everyday words including most of the irregular verbs and nouns with irregular plurals of the **man-men**, **mouse-mice**, **child-children** type. These words are usually short, vague and general such as **thing**, **people** and sometimes even many slangy and colloquial words like **guys**, **bucks**. Students are not suggested to use these words, even in speaking. It is enough just to understand them. There are also expressions like **well**, **I mean**, **you know**, which should be used sparingly.

1.5.2 Correct and effective sentence structure

Differences exist between spoken English and written English in the way words are put together to make sentences, particularly in the relation between grammatical functions and semantic roles. Compare the sentences below:

c.f.
- *Laszlo Biro invented the ball-point pen.*
- *The ball-point pen was invented by Laszlo Biro.*
- *Laszlo Biro's invention of ball-point pen was a great contribution to our life.*

Item		Spoken English	Written English
Sentence building	Subject	doer of action	doer/receiver/action/state/ quality
	Predicate	action (active voice)	action (active voice / passive voice) / verb (of abstract meaning)
	Object	receiver of action	receiver of action/ by doer
Subject		a personal pronoun: *I, you, she, he, it, we, they*	an abstract noun denoting an action, state, quality, etc.
		a noun referring to a person or something concrete	a noun clause
		"*it*" used to refer to time, weather or in patterns such as "*It's easy to...*"	an infinitive phrase
Action		in active voice	transitive verbs in passive voice
			verbs as subject, object...
			verbs in noun form

Ex. 1-5-2-1 *Revise the following sentences into more formal written English; select a suitable word to be the subject.*

1. I felt very happy after that.
2. I was very nervous, so I couldn't sleep well.
3. Every person needs to give and receive love.
4. The first time I saw the sea, I was very disappointed.
5. After climbing a flight of stairs we came to the top.
6. If people are not healthy, they can't enjoy a happy life.
7. I couldn't concentrate on my studies. This situation worried me even more.

1.5.3　Figures of speech

Words used in their original meanings are used literally, while words used in extended meanings for the purpose of making comparisons or calling up pictures in the reader's or listener's mind are used figuratively. In *"a colorful garden,"* the word *"colorful"* is used in its literal sense, but in *"a colorful life"* and *"a colorful career,"* the word *"colorful"* is used in its figurative sense. Neither life nor career has any color; *"colorful"* here has a new, extended or figurative meaning, i.e. exciting, interesting and rich in variety. The word suggests a comparison between life or career and something that has different colors, like a garden, and because of this association, the word is more impressive than a word used in its literal sense, such as interesting and exciting.

There are various ways of using words figuratively. They are called figures of speech. Among the most common of them are:

1. Simile

A simile is a comparison between two distinctly different things and the comparison is indicated by the word *"as"* or *"like."*

e.g.
O my love's like a red, red rose.
The old man's hair is as white as snow.
Practice: _____

2. Metaphor

A metaphor is the use of a word which originally denotes one thing to refer to another with a similar quality. It is also a comparison, but the comparison is implied, not expressed with the word *"as"* or *"like."* Metaphors are not only used after the verb *"to be,"* nouns can also be used metaphorically.

e.g.
*He is the **soul** of the team.*
*The street **faded** into a country road with **straggling** houses by it.*
Practice: _____

3. Personification

Personification is to treat a thing or an idea as if it were human or had human qualities. It is commonly used in poetry.

e.g.
*The match will soon be over and defeat is **staring** at us in the face.*
*Thunder **roared** and a **pouring** rain started.*

Practice: _____

4. Metonymy

Metonymy is substituting the name of one thing for another with which it is closely associated. Thus, the crown can stand for a king, the White House for the American government, the bottle for wine or alcohol, and the bar for the legal profession. When metonymy is well used, brevity and vividness can be achieved.

e.g.

*When the war was over, he laid down the sword and took up the **pen**.*

*His **purse** would not allow him the luxury.*

Practice: _____

5. Synecdoche

Synecdoche is to substitute a part for the whole, or the whole for a part.

e.g.

*The farms were short of **hands** during the harvest season.*

*He has to **earn his daily bread** by doing odd jobs.*

Practice: _____

6. Euphemism

Euphemism is the substitution of a mild or vague expression for a harsh or unpleasant one.

e.g.

to die: *to pass away; to leave us; one's heart has stopped beating*

old people: *senior citizens*

mad: *emotionally disturbed*

Practice: _____

7. Irony

Irony is the use of words which are clearly opposite to what is meant, in order to achieve a special effect. Suppose you planned an outing on a certain day, expecting it to be fine. But when the day came, it was raining heavily. If you said, *"What a fine weather for an outing!,"* you were using an irony. If a barbarous act is described as civilized or cultural, irony is also used.

Practice: _____

8. Overstatement and understatement

Overstatement refers to the act of speaking more than the truth, exaggerating the subject. Understatement, on the other hand, refers to the act of speaking less than the truth, playing down the magnitude or value of the subject.

    e.g.

    She is **dying** to know what job has been assigned to her.

    It took **a few dollars** to build this indoor swimming pool.

    Practice: _____

9. Transferred epithet

An epithet is an adjective or a descriptive phrase that serves to characterize somebody or something. A transferred epithet is one that is shifted from the noun it logically modifies to a word associated with that noun.

    e.g.

    She was so worried about her son that she had spent several **sleepless** nights.

    In his **quiet** laziness, he suddenly remembered that strange word.

    Practice: _____

10. Oxymoron

In an oxymoron, some apparently contradictory terms are combined to produce a special effect.

    e.g.

    The coach had to be **cruel to be kind** to his trainees.

    She read the long-waited letter with **a tearful smile**.

    Practice: _____

1.6 Words

In the preface of *The Right Word at the Right Time*, the author gives a vivid description of the importance of using the right words: "Using the right word at the right time is rather like wearing appropriate clothing for the occasion: it is a courtesy to others, and a favor to yourself—a matter of presenting yourself well in the eyes of the world."

As the "building blocks" of writing, words play the first and foremost role in writing. In some cases, it is just the mastery of words that constitutes the foundation for communication in language.

1.6.1 Denotation vs. connotation

The meaning of a word is comprehensive. If we are asked to describe a person who is old, we always have to decide whether the word "*old*" is the proper one. If the person is a respectable teacher, we may not use it for its unpleasant overtone. This implication of a word is called **connotation**.

Denotation, on the other hand, refers to the literal meaning, the one or the actual dictionary definition of the word, without the attachment of an emotional response. However, in all kinds of writing, the words we choose may do more than the literal meaning. The selection of a word often tells how the writer feels about the subject. Many words, though similar in their denotation, may reveal quite different attitudes of the writer, i.e. connotation. To this end, when we write in English, we have to be very careful with such emotionally loaded words.

Ex. 1-6-1-1 *Fill in the table and study the denotations and connotations.*

Word	Denotation	Connotation	Sentence
	symbol *Au*, a soft, yellow, corrosion-resistant element		
blood			Blood is thicker than water.
	the female parent	protectiveness, affection	
weed			Don't be such a weed!

1.6.2 Better words

The success of writing depends, to a large extent, on the fluent language. There are three criteria of good word choice: conciseness, preciseness and effectiveness.

1. Conciseness

An expression should be simple and free of unnecessary words. However, wordiness is not always easy to spot. The best way to avoid wordiness is to read the writing carefully and try to find words, phrases or even sentences that are not essential and delete them.

2. Preciseness

An expression should be specific rather than general.

3. Effectiveness

Effectiveness is based on the first two qualities and refers to the skillful use of language that adds power to our writing.

Ex. 1-6-2-1 *Fill in the blanks with the proper words given.*
1. small/little
   What a sweet _____ girl!
   He packed his belongings in a _____ bag.
2. childlike/childish
   She followed him with _____ trust.
   I am tired of your _____ words.

3. modest/humble

The young composer is very _____ about his success.

This man was especially _____ while talking with the superiors.

4. cheap/inexpensive

Buying _____ electronic appliances is not a good idea in the long run.

Her clothes, though made of _____ material, are quite elegant.

5. economical/mean

He is too _____ with his money to donate even a penny to the charities.

She is quite a(n) _____ manager and runs the company smoothly.

Ex. 1-6-2-2 *Read the following passage and choose the more suitable word from the two options provided for each blank.*

Until she was five years old, Jade Snow's world was almost wholly Chinese, for her world was her _____ (home, family), the Wongs. Life was secure but formal, sober but quietly _____ (happy, glad) and the few _____ (questions, problems) she had were entirely concerned with what was _____ (appropriate, proper) or improper in the behavior of a _____ (small, little) Chinese girl.

Even at this _____ (small, early) age she had _____ (learned, studied) the meaning of discipline, without understanding the necessity for it. A little girl never _____ (asked, questioned) the commands of Mother and Father, unless prepared to receive painful _____ (effects, consequences). She never addressed an older person by name—it was always Elder Brother, Eldest Sister, Second Elder Sister, Third Elder Sister (she had died at one month without a name, but still she held a place in the _____ (home, family), and Fourth Elder Sister. Only her mother and father, or their generation of uncles and aunts, addressed them as Blessing from Heaven, Jade Swallow, Jade Lotus or Jade Ornament. In short, a little girl was never casual with her _____ (olders, elders). Even in handing them something, she must use both hands to signify that she _____ (held, paid) them undivided attention.

1.7 Sentences

The basic unit of a paragraph is the sentence. A sentence, as the linguist Donald Hall defines, is a group of words with a period, exclamation points or a question mark at the end.

1.7.1 Basic qualities of good sentences

It is the well-constructed sentences that express complete thoughts or ideas most effectively. A good sentence should have four basic qualities: unity, coherence, conciseness and emphasis.

1. Unity

Unity is the first essential element of sentence structure. A unified sentence is the expression of a single complete thought in words and therefore, it produces a single effect.

A sentence violates the principle of unity if it contains ideas that are not closely related. To put it in other words, a sentence is not unified if it does not express a complete thought.

c.f.

His daughter was about fifteen, and I was talking to him when she arrived.
While I was talking to him, his daughter, a girl about fifteen, arrived.

2. Coherence

Coherence deals with the relationships which link the meanings of utterances in a discourse or of the sentences in a text. In writing a paragraph, coherence is achieved when a series of sentences develop the main idea of the paragraph.

A sentence is coherent when its words or parts are properly connected and their relationships are made unmistakably clear. Coherence is violated when there are such faults as faulty parallel constructions, ambiguous reference of pronouns, dangling or misplaced modifiers, confusing shifts, mixed or incomplete constructions, etc.

c.f.

*He likes to swim, to ski and basketball.
He likes to swim, to ski and to play basketball.

3. Conciseness

Conciseness helps to make a sentence effective. When two versions express the same idea, the shorter one is usually the better. To achieve conciseness, one should avoid wordiness and unnecessary repetition. Compare the following pairs of sentences:

c.f.

Smith was in no position to argue against knowledgeable doctors or what the medical textbook says.
Smith has no qualifications to argue against the medical authorities.

4. Emphasis

A well-unified and coherently-constructed sentence should be emphatic enough. Important ideas in sentences can be emphasized in many ways, as are discussed later (1.7.4).

1.7.2 How to write correct sentences

To structure an English sentence correctly, we must follow several principles.

1. Subject-predicate agreement

Verbs must agree in person and number with their subjects. The following rules present the usage of subject-predicate agreement.

- When the subject is a plural, the predicate (verb) is used in plural form.
- When the subject contains words such as *"either ... or"* and *"neither ... nor,"* the verb must agree with the number of the part closest to it.
- When the subject is an indefinite pronoun ending in *"body," "one"* and *"thing,"* the verb is used singularly. A noun with *"both of," "few of"* and *"many of"* requires the verb to be in plural form. A noun with *"all of," "most of," "none of"* and *"some of"* requires the verb to be used singularly or plurally, depending on the noun that follows.
- When the subject is a relative pronoun (*who, which, that, what*) with no number of its own, it takes its number from the antecedent it refers to. A relative pronoun referring to a single antecedent needs a verb in singular form, and a relative pronoun referring to a plural antecedent needs a verb in plural form.
- When the subject is a collective noun, such as *"society," "police," "machinery," "audience," "family," "committee"* or *"crew,"* the verb can be either singular or plural depending on whether the group named is acting as a single unit or as a number of separate individuals.
- When the subject is a seemingly plural but actually a singular noun ending in *"s"* (such as *"maths," "boss"*), the verb is used singularly.

2. Pronoun-antecedent agreement

Pronouns may be of great help in avoiding unnecessary repetition, but they may also be a source of errors in writing. Their agreement with antecedents is the key to their usage.

When used improperly, the writing may be confusing or misleading. So make sure that each of the pronouns used refers clearly to one word and does not force the reader to guess the meaning it signifies. The following sentences are examples with misused pronouns.

The cat scratched **her eye with **her** claw. (Note: the first HER may/may not apply to the cat.)*

John's father told John that **he was supposed to paint the garage doors on Sunday.* (Note: *"he"* may refer to either *"John's father"* or *"John."*)

To avoid the confusion, it is advisable not to overuse pronouns; it is better to have a longer sentence than a confusing shorter one. When necessary, repeating a person's name twice in one sentence may be better than *his, hers* or *theirs* to replace the noun or name.

3. Parallelism

Equal elements and ideas should be balanced in parallel structures. This means that two words or phrases, if equal in value, should be expressed in the same grammatical forms. Parallel structures prevent confusion, lead to clarity and are often more economical.

Parallelism is the writer's technique of balancing the like with the like—nouns with nouns, verbs with verbs, infinitives with infinitives, prepositional phrases with prepositional phrases, and so forth. In many ways, parallelism can help the readers move forward easily from one idea to the next.

Whenever you list a series of things, actions or ideas, you should equally express them. Otherwise, you merely make your ideas difficult for the readers to understand.

4. Dangling and misplaced modifiers

A modifier must clearly and sensibly modify a word or group of words. It is usually placed close to the word it modifies. If this criterion has not been met, it is called a dangling modifier.

Some introductory verbal phrases such as *"to tell the truth," "to begin with," "judging from," "considering…," "generally speaking," "provided that …,"* etc. are all well established and do not need to be attached to particular subjects.

1.7.3 How to write effective sentences

1. Use more active voice when necessary

Whether it is more appropriate to use the active or the passive voice depends on the context or on what the writer intends to emphasize.

However, the active voice is in general preferable to the passive, and is more frequently used in English writing because it makes the writing more concise and vigorous.

The passive voice is considered to be more appropriate when:

(1) The receiver of the action is more important than the doer.

(2) The writer wishes to emphasize the receiver.

(3) The doer of the action is unknown or hard to identify.

(4) The writer does not want to reveal his or her identity.

2. Avoid choppy sentences

Sometimes a simple idea is broken up unnecessarily into two or more sentences. A succession of such short sentences produces an abrupt, jerky effect and obstructs the flow of thought, for the sentences fail to show the relationship between ideas. The way to avoid such a choppy style is to join the related ideas into one sentence by using appropriate transitional words.

3. Be prudent in using the expletives

"There" and *"it"* are called expletives as "filling" words and placed at the beginning of a sentence to put emphasis on the subject of a sentence. As a rhetorical device, this placement has the effect of suspending the sentence.

e.g.

There are a few chairs around the table.

It is not my intention to hurt his feelings.

In the above examples, the actual subjects are *"chair"* in the first sentence and *"to hurt his feelings"* in the second. These two subjects are given a certain degree of emphasis, because the expletives *"there"* and *"it"* delay their appearance in the sentences. Expletives can be most effective in some contexts.

4. Avoid run-on sentences

Sentences which are carelessly strung together by using *"and," "but," "so," "then"* are called stringy sentences or run-on sentences. A run-on sentence often results from combining too many independent clauses into one sentence. Tacked together in this way, the sentence becomes not only childish and monotonous, but also ineffective. We can improve it by subordinating ideas of less importance or by separating the sentence into two or more shorter ones.

5. Be careful with loose sentences and periodic sentences

A loose sentence is one in which the main idea is stated near or at the beginning, and is then followed by details. A periodic sentence is one in which the main idea is held in suspense till the end of the sentence.

The loose sentence is a characteristic structure of spoken English and is most commonly used in both speaking and writing. In expressing ideas, we naturally put the important point first and then add whatever we want to say. In a loose sentence, the main idea comes first, followed by the modifying clauses or phrases to qualify, explain, amplify or alter its meaning. The periodic sentence needs planning beforehand and is not widely used in the end, which is an effective means to achieve emphasis.

1.7.4 How to achieve emphasis in a sentence

Emphasis is a Latin word, meaning *"force of expression."* Sentence emphasis means the arrangement of words in a sentence in such a way that the important information may receive the best attention.

1. Make use of subordination and combination

A succession of short sentences may lead to choppy style that leaves no emphasis among different ideas. By using subordination or combination, the important ideas will be emphasized and thus more effective.

To join short sentences into one, we need decide which ideas are more stressed or unstressed. Ideas improperly placed confuse and mislead the readers.

2. Pay attention to the information focus in a sentence

To give proper emphasis to a sentence, we need to follow these two general rules:

1) Put the least important information in the middle.

2) Leave the most important information at the end.

Generally speaking, the beginning and end of a sentence are the best places for putting the information a writer wants to emphasize. Among the three positions—the beginning, the middle and the end—the most prominent is the end. Next comes the beginning, and the middle is the least important.

3. Learn to invert word order

We may invert the normal order of a sentence to achieve emphasis. Usually it is used to propose the intended information focus.

4. Climax with the word order

The word "climax" comes from the Greek word "klimax," meaning *ladder*. Climax is a means by which the different propositions of a sentence are made to ascend from the lower to the higher. It is a rising arrangement with the chief interest placed at the end.

By contrast, anticlimax is a drop from the most important to the least important. It may be done intentionally to create a humorous effect.

e.g.

I lost my bag and with it, my wallet, my ID card and my dirty socks.

The sudden transition from more valuable things to *"dirty socks"* produces some humorous effect.

Used in a proper place, the anticlimax can create unexpected effects. In this way, emphasis on certain ideas is more successfully achieved.

5. Repetition

Careless repetition indicates a poor mastery of vocabulary and weakens the effectiveness of a sentence. But the careful use of it can create emphasis and clarity.

6. Parallelism

Parallelism consists of phrases or sentences of similar construction placed side by side, often balancing each other. It is a means by which similar ideas are expressed in similar grammatical forms.

Tips:
- Use parallel structures for coordinate sentence elements;
- Use parallel sentences for correlatives like ***"both…and,"*** ***"either…or,"*** ***"neither…nor,"*** *"not only … but also"*;
- Repeat to make the parallel structures more emphatic;
- Avoid faulty parallelism—similar ideas can be achieved through different organizations of words.

---

7. Rhetorical questions

A rhetorical question differs from the ordinary question in that it does not need an answer.

Readers may pause and reflect for a moment when they come upon a rhetorical question, thus creating an emphasis in their minds. The famous words by Shelly in his *Ode to the West Wind*, "If winter comes, can spring be far behind?" wouldn't have been so effective without the use of rhetorical questions.

A positive rhetorical question equals a strong negative statement, while a negative rhetorical question equals a strong positive statement.

Ex. 1-7-1 *Fill in the blanks with the proper forms of the words given in the brackets.*
   1. More than half of the city _____ (be) affected by the flood.
   2. War and peace _____ (remain) a constant theme in history.
   3. Sufficient data _____ (have) been collected.
   4. The Philippines _____ (lie) to the south-east of China.
   5. The singer and dancer _____ (intend) to attend our evening party.
   6. Three weeks _____ (allow) for making the preparation.
   7. There _____ (be) a pen, a knife and several books on the desk.
   8. The shelf full of books and magazines _____ (stand) in the corner of the room.

Ex. 1-7-2 *Correct the following faulty sentences.*
   1. On arriving at the airport, a speech was made by the president.
   2. To be well-informed, reading extensively is necessary.
   3. Astronauts must be intelligent, cool-headed and have exceptional health.
   4. Jack decided to get a job rather than going to the university.
   5. Listening carefully to what does the teacher say in class saves work later.
   6. After the traffic accident, I opened my eyes slowly and realized whether I was still alive.

Ex. 1-7-3 *Rewrite and polish up the following sentences.*
   1. Listening attentively, the mistake was found.
   2. Since she believed the ship could be saved, she called for volunteers to help him.
   3. It makes me feel painful to think that she has to work twelve hours a day and seven days a week.
   4. When what the speaker was saying was not audible to our ears, I asked him to repeat again what he had said.
   5. Suzhou is where one can find some 2,000 pavilions and towers.
   6. China's civilization is one of the world's oldest civilizations.
   7. He was selfless, diligent and honest; that's why he became a great scientist.
   8. She had been confined to bed for a long time. This had impaired the function of her ankles.
   9. If we study Mars carefully through a telescope, we will see a number of dark, blue-green markings.

Chapter Two
Paragraph Writing

Introduction

A paragraph is a unit of organization of written language which serves to indicate how the main ideas in a written text are grouped. A paragraph should develop one central idea or express one unit of thought and be unified, coherent and well-built by linking all its related sentences together. There are many ways or techniques to develop a paragraph, and the choice is based on the content of the paragraph and the intention of the writer.

2.1 Paragraph Structure

A paragraph is like a sandwich, with the topic and concluding sentence as the two pieces of "bread" and the supporting sentences as the "meat" in-between.

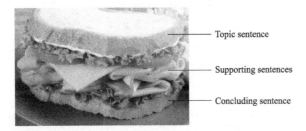

A regular paragraph has three important parts:

- **Topic sentence:** A topic sentence tells what topic the paragraph is going to discuss;
- **Supporting sentences:** The supporting sentences give details about the topic;
- **Concluding sentence:** The concluding sentence summarizes the main points of the paragraph or restates the topic sentence in different words.

2.1.1 Topic sentence

e.g.

I need a water bottle for the hike in case I get thirsty. A sweater is useful if it gets cold. A compass will help me go in the right direction. Sandwiches will be an easy-to-carry snack. I can use a camera to take pictures of unusual or attractive places.

Is this a paragraph?

The answer is definitely not. Without a central idea, a group of sentences is just a list rather than an actual paragraph. However, we can make it a paragraph by giving it a central idea or a focus, which is called the topic sentence.

e.g.

I need many items to be ready for a safe and enjoyable hike. *I need a water bottle for the hike in case I get thirsty. A sweater is useful if it gets cold. A compass will help me go in the right direction. Sandwiches will be an easy-to-carry snack. I can use a camera to take pictures of unusual or attractive places. Therefore, convenient items are indispensable for me to enjoy my hike.*

A carefully thought-out topic sentence will serve two important functions.　It will:

● provide the writers with the means to stay focused on their objective; (It's a lot easier to write if they know what they are going to write about.)

● offer the readers the tools they need to clearly understand what the writers have to say.

Functioning as the most important sentence in a paragraph, the topic sentence consists of two parts: a topic and a controlling idea. The topic refers to the subject of the paragraph while the controlling idea tells what the paragraph will say about the topic and limits the topic to a very specific point.

There are some rules for topic sentence as follows.

● Topic sentence should be a complete sentence with a complete meaning.

e.g.

*How to read a novel.

We may use this fragment as a title rather than a topic sentence unless we correct it as a complete sentence:

e.g.

Anyone can learn how to read a novel.

● Topic sentence should be neither too general nor too specific.

e.g.

*Digital cameras take photos.

This is too general because there is no specific controlling idea. The reader cannot tell what the paragraph will say about the digital cameras except their basic functions.

e.g.

*Digital photos are composed of small squares, just like a tiled kitchen floor or bathroom wall.

This is too specific because it gives information which is too detailed to be developed later in the paragraph.

e.g.

Digital cameras have several advantages over film cameras.

This is a good topic sentence, for it gives the reader a hint about what the paragraph will discuss later. A good topic sentence tells something about the contents of the paragraph but none of the details.

2.1.2 Concluding sentence

A concluding sentence signals the end of a paragraph and reminds the reader of the main idea again. Here are three tips to write a good concluding sentence.

- Begin the sentence with a concluding signal, such as *"in conclusion," "in short," "indeed," "in brief," "in summary," "to conclude," "to summarize," "to sum up," "all in all,"* ...
- Remind the reader of the main idea by repeating the idea in the topic sentence or summarizing the main points of the paragraph.
- Never introduce a new idea in the concluding sentence!

2.1.3 Supporting sentences

The supporting sentences explain the topic by giving more information about the topic sentence, i.e. they list the main points of a paragraph.

2.2 Ways to Enhance Coherence

A good paragraph has coherence. The sentences are sequenced according to a clear and logical plan of development. To gain coherence, many writers decide before writing how they will build each paragraph.

2.2.1 Listing

Listing is a powerful way to demonstrate a series of observations and to emphasize each element. By listing in paragraphs when you want to itemize or list a set of topics or a series of some kind, the writer can analyze causes and effects, state the importance of something, or list the shortcomings or benefits. Listing can also be used to refute opponents' ideas or to state personal opinions.

Most often, listing mode starts with a general statement and proceeds to details. In other words, the paragraph starts with a topic sentence that states a point of view and then provides discussions usually ordered from the most important idea to the less important to the least important, or *vice versa*.

There are several points that are worth our attention when we build a paragraph by listing.

First, arrange the supporting ideas in a logical order. It is essential that we should arrange the supporting details in a logical order in everything we write. Otherwise, paragraphs are not effective or cannot be best followed by readers. Chinese students, when writing in English, tend to focus all their attention on expressing ideas and thus ignore the arrangement of the ideas.

Second, we should pay attention to the correct use of listing expressions. The following bank offers the possible expressions used for listing.

> *the first point; first; firstly; first of all; to begin with; primarily; initially; other points; second; secondly; next; the next; then; moreover; furthermore; in addition; for the other; another; the other; last; the last; lastly; in the end; finally; the final; last but not the least...*

Remember the following rules when using these expressions:
- Don't mix sets of listing expressions;
- Distinguish "*first*" from "*at first*." "*First*" is a listing word, but "*at first*" indicates a change;
- Distinguish "*last*" from "*at last*." "*Last*" is a listing word, but "*at last*" indicates that something happens after a long expectation.

Ex. 2-2-1-1 *Develop the following topic sentence into a complete paragraph by using the listing mode.*

Some people disagree with the statement that the use of private cars should be greatly encouraged in China now, especially in large cities. Their main reasons are as follows.

_____
_____
_____
_____
_____
_____

Ex. 2-2-1-2 *Develop the following topic sentence into a complete paragraph by using the listing mode.*

The Internet is very popular among the Chinese. Many people like shopping online for various reasons.

_____
_____
_____

2.2.2 Classification

To classify is to sort things into categories according to their differing characteristics. One group of items may be classified in different ways; it all depends on the reason for making the classification. To find out the make-up of students in the department, for instance, the department office might classify the students according to the grades they got in the last final examinations. Or it might classify them on the basis of their interests.

Below are some of the possible expressions about classification.

Noun	*kind; class; type; category; aspect; section; part; division*
Verb	*classify; divide; fall into; group into; distinguish from; distinct*
Adjective	*distinguished; distinctive; similar; namely; contradictory; opposite; basic; fundamental; significant; primary; secondary*
Phrase	*the first kind; the second type; major category*

Ex. 2-2-2-1 *Look at the following diagram. It is a tree diagram classification of drinks. Write a paragraph to describe the classification of it based upon the information in the diagram.*

Drinks may be classified into two main groups:

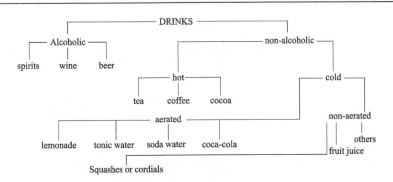

Ex. 2-2-2-2 *Write about the different kinds of universities and colleges in China.*

Suggested words:

leading universities; provincial key universities; local college; comprehensive; science and engineering; foreign languages; humanities; public and private

2.2.3 Cause and effect

A cause and effect paragraph describes the causes that have produced a certain effect—the reasons why a particular outcome has occurred. To use this technique effectively, you must convince the readers that the causes given are both necessary and sufficient to produce the effect or effects we have indicated. In other words, you should make the relationship between the cause and the effect clear to the reader.

The organization of a paragraph by cause and effect can be accomplished in two ways:
- Begin the paragraph with an effect and then list the causes of the effect;
- Begin with the causes and then list their effect or effects.

If the writer's objective is to show why something exists or occurs, then the effect-to-cause is the better choice. If the writer's goal is to show the consequences, then the cause-to-effect order is more appropriate.

Whatever orders the writer chooses, he/she must follow basic paragraph format. That is, begin with a topic sentence and then present the specific supporting details.

Fact statements and reason explanations on why or how the facts come about are the basic procedure in paragraph development by cause and effect.

Conjunction	because; owing to; due to; as a result; because of; so; therefore; thus; consequently; for this reason; since; for; as; on account of; as a consequence; accordingly; hence; in view of; on the ground that; out of
Verb	cause; produce; generate; lead to; result from; result in; bring about; have an effect on; give rise to; induce; contribute to

Ex. 2-2-3-1 *Reorder the following sentences for a complete paragraph.*

1. Paris grew because it was the only city in France where anyone could arrive and know he could at least survive, perhaps prosper.

2. Three factors contributed to this population explosion.

3. The increase was also due in part to the general peace and prosperity of the Second Empire.

4. The increase was partly the result of better health conditions.

5. But the city's population rise came about mainly because the railroads carried the promise of

Paris to rural France.

6. From 1851 to 1872, the number of Parisians nearly doubled—from 1,242,000 to 2,212,000.

Ex. 2-2-3-2 *Develop the following topic sentence into a complete paragraph by adopting the cause and effect mode.*

> **Suggested words and expressions:**
> *individuality; atmosphere; relieve the pressure*

There are several reasons for the boom in celebrating foreign festivals on Chinese campuses.

_____
_____
_____
_____
_____

2.2.4 Comparison and contrast

Comparison and contrast are often used in paragraph or essay writing. The difference between the two is that comparison shows the similarities between two or more people, places, objects or ideas, while contrast shows the differences or dissimilarities between the items compared.

In general, people like to compare two things that are similar in some ways and different in others. When we compare and contrast, we tell how things are similar and different. Two things can be similar and yet dissimilar at the same time. Often, we put together a lot of information that is of the same kind or class, and then we are interested in looking at the differences in detail. In other words, we start with a comparison that is already made and focus our attention on the contrast.

There are two major ways of organizing paragraphs of comparison and contrast. One is to examine one thing thoroughly and then start the other. The other is to examine two things at the same time, discussing them point by point.

When using comparison or contrast to develop a paragraph, pay attention to the following rules:

- Both comparison and contrast need a specific dominant quality, point or issue (controlling idea) by which we will be governed in the selection of basic material.
- Comparison deals only with similarities.
- Contrast deals only with dissimilarities.
- Both require that material be placed in some predetermined order for good coherence.

The following phrases and sentence patterns are often used in developing comparison and contrast paragraphs.

Words & Phrases	on the contrary; in contrast; in comparison; on the other hand; be like; just as; be the same as; similarly; likewise; while; whereas; yet; but; however; differently
Sentence Pattern	1. There are some (a few, many) differences (similarities) between A and B. 2. A differs from B (is different from B) in three aspects. 3. A has something (much) in common with B. 4. A has some advantages over B. 5. Let us make a comparison (contrast) between A and B. 6. We can easily compare A with B, and see the differences and similarities between them. 7. One difference (similarity) seems to be (lies in; is) that ...

Ex. 2-2-4-1 *Fill in the blanks with proper conjunctions for a fluent paragraph.*

Speech and writing are different in many ways. Speech depends on sounds; writing, _____, uses written symbols. Speech was developed about 500,000 years ago, _____ written language is a recent development, which was invented only about 6,000 years ago. Speech is usually informal, _____ word choice of writing, _____, is often relatively formal. _____ pronunciation and accent often tell where the speaker is from, they are ignored in writing because a standard diction and spelling system prevails in most countries. Speech relies on gesture, loudness and the rise and fall of the voice, _____ writing lacks these features. Careful speakers and writers can be aware of the differences.

Ex. 2-2-4-2 *Contrast between the different modes of traveling in China.*

Suggested words and expressions:
package tour; individual travel; convenience; freedom

_____
_____
_____
_____

2.2.5 Exemplification

A very general statement is seldom impressive or convincing. It is usually necessary to give examples to prove, to illustrate or to clarify a general statement. We may be too accustomed to saying "for instance" or "for example" to realize that we are using a certain technique or method to develop a topic.

Another way to organize sentences into a paragraph is describing in detail. This is a method that we use almost every time we talk about our own experience, about a piece of news or about a historical event. We usually start with a general statement, which is like a topic sentence, and then we may add some description or explanation.

This kind of paragraph writing technique is similar to exemplification. There may be cases where a fine distinction between description and exemplification is difficult to make. When details are presented for their own sake, as in the description of an accident, the way is to develop a paragraph in detail. If details are chosen to illustrate a general point, as in explaining by a certain dictionary, they become examples. In other words, details themselves are important in the method of "description" while the general statement is emphasized in the technique of "exemplification." The commonly applied expressions to introduce exemplifications are labeled in the following bank.

---

for example; for instance; to illustrate; take ... for example; as an example; as a case in point; as a final example; cite as proof; according to the statistics; according to the statistical evidence; such as.

Ex. 2-2-5-1 *Develop the following topic sentence into a complete paragraph by using the strategy of exemplification.*

Presently, there are many means of transportation for people to travel by. One of the best, for example,

_____

_____

_____

My favorite means of transport is

_____

_____

_____

Ex. 2-2-5-2 *Develop the following topic sentence into a complete paragraph by employing the mode of exemplification.*

Suggested words and expressions:
wallpaper; plastic flowers; pictures; rearrange; furniture

Decorating a dormitory room is a challenge.

PART TWO
COMPOSING ESSAYS

Introduction

The structure of an essay is similar to that of a paragraph. Just as the controlling idea of a paragraph is expressed in the topic sentence, the controlling idea of an essay is expressed in the thesis statement. The topic sentence of a paragraph is generally placed at the beginning of the paragraph, and the thesis statement of an essay is generally placed in the introductory paragraph. In both paragraphs and essays, specific supports in the form of facts, details and examples are needed to validate the opinion expressed in the controlling idea. Finally, both paragraphs and essays tend to restate the controlling idea at the end of the discussion.

Apart from the fact that the length of an essay is longer than that of a paragraph, the difference between a paragraph and an essay mainly lies in development. A paragraph usually deals with only one dimension of a topic, while an essay discusses a subject through several dimensions. Since the complexity of the subject demands more than a one-paragraph treatment, the paragraphs of an essay deal with a sequence of key points, each focusing on one key point.

Major Parts of an Essay

Generally speaking, there are three major sections in every essay: the introduction, the main body and the conclusion.

1. Introduction

The introductory paragraph should accomplish two tasks:
- It should prepare the reader for the discussion or get the reader's interest so that he/she wants to read more.
- It should let the reader know what the writing is going to be about.

The introduction usually starts with a general discussion of the subject and leads to a very specific statement of the writer's main point or the thesis. Sometimes an essay begins with a

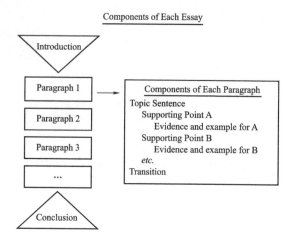

challenging claim or a surprising story to catch the readers' attention. The beginning sentences can present some background information about the topic, the situation of the issue or different opinions of the discussion. The thesis statement is a sentence (or two) that states what the writer is going to do in the essay. It is a kind of signpost or map that shows the reader what direction the writer will take. It usually comes at the end of the introduction.

Look at the following samples of introduction:

Does Space Exploration Benefit Mankind?

Some countries spend billions of dollars on space research each year. For many people, space really is the final frontier. They are excited by the exploration and potential of space. However, not everyone agrees that this money is well-spent. Many people feel that we should solve problems here on Earth before beginning our journey to space. I am convinced that space exploration is justified.

Are Zoos Cruel to Wild Animals?

Many people have had their first experience of animals from visiting zoos as children and feel that they are important for education and conservation. However, others feel that zoos are stressful and cruel to animals. This essay will discuss the importance of zoos and their essential role in conserving endangered wildlife.

Does Aid to Poor Countries Work?

For the last fifty years, the impoverished countries have been receiving millions of dollars from affluent donor countries. Some of this money has improved lives, while much of it does not reach the needy. In this essay, I am going to outline the arguments against foreign aid.

2. Main body

The main body may consist of several paragraphs. Each body paragraph will focus on a single idea, reason or example that supports the thesis. Each paragraph will have a clear topic sentence and as much discussion or explanation as is necessary to explain the point. Details and specific examples are employed to make the ideas clear and convincing.

Since each body paragraph deals with one aspect or dimension of the thesis, it is not effective to simply jump from one idea to the next. Therefore, transitions are employed to connect the paragraphs to one another. The writer needs to use the end of one paragraph and/or the beginning of the next to show the relationship between the two ideas. If the first paragraph tells a pro and the second a con, the writer can use "on the other hand, ..." If the second paragraph tells something of greater significance, the writer can use "More importantly, ..."

Look at the following sample of body paragraphs:

Suitability is the Key to a Good Job

*For many, a good job means a good salary and a high social position. I don't agree. In my opinion, it is better to regard "good" as meaning the job is suitable to your personality (**topic sentence**). For example, if you are the withdrawn type, it may be more suitable for you to do academic research in a university than to work in a foreign enterprise, because the latter requires an outgoing and sociable personality. Maybe it is not easy for the introverted to do that sort of job well. Additionally, if you get a job which fits your personality, you will more likely succeed in it.*

*Furthermore, a good job means one which is also suitable to your interests (**topic sentence**). That is to say, you can get enjoyment from doing it. If you don't enjoy your job, even if it gives you a very good salary and high social position, you can't really lead a happy and meaningful life. We should work to live, not live to work.*

*Also, a good job should mean a suitable chance to improve yourself as a person (**topic sentence**). As the famous saying goes: One is never too old to learn. So you should improve yourself while you work. In other words, your job should provide you with challenges so that you can develop yourself.*

3. Conclusion

The conclusion usually begins with a restatement of the main point; but the writer should be sure to paraphrase, not just repeat the thesis sentence. Sometimes the writer may want to add some sentences that emphasize the importance of the topic and the significance of the point. The conclusion is the reverse of the introduction in that it starts out very specific and becomes a bit more general as it finishes.

Look at the following samples of conclusion:

Good Manners

If everyone has developed good manners, people will form a more harmonious relation. If everyone behaves considerately towards others, people will live in a better world. With the general mood of society improved, there will be a progress of civilization.

Should We Test Products on Animals?

I agree that we need to make sure that animals who are used for testing new products have the minimum of suffering. However, I am convinced that animal testing is necessary, and that it will continue to benefit humans in new and wonderful ways.

Types of Essays

There are different categories of writing, each having a specific purpose. Whatever you want to call them, modes of writing, forms of writing, types of writing or domains of writing, there are basically four modes: narration, description, exposition and argumentation. However, by this classification it is not meant that there is only one mode in a certain piece of writing. Actually, in most writings, these modes are mixed in natural combinations; for example, narration frequently includes description.

Questions to think about before you start writing

1. What is the purpose of the essay?
2. Who is the target audience?
3. Does anything need to be clarified or explained to the audience?
4. What kind of writing and degree of formality are best suited?

Chapter Three

Narration

Introduction

The narrative mode can be found in some form within many of the other modes, but it can be used by itself as well. When it is used by itself, the narrative mode tells a story by describing a sequence of events or actions. In its broadest sense, it includes stories (real or imaginary), biographies, histories, news items and narrative poems. When students write a narrative, they usually narrate their personal experiences.

Usually, narration includes the conventions of storytelling: plot, character, setting, climax and ending. In composing a piece of narration, great attention should be paid to the organization of the story and the details of the story.

3.1 Employment of Various Points of View

The narrator of your story is the voice that is telling the story. For example, read the same scene described by three different narrators:

— *I pulled out the gun and showed it to the cute blond bank teller, who gave a little yelp of surprise.*

— *This bald guy came up to my counter and reached into his jacket. Suddenly, I realized he was holding a gun.*

— *A bald jerk cut in front of me in line. I hate cutters, so I was about to go say something, when he pulled a gun on the blond lady behind the counter.*

All of these examples use first person narrators. That means the narrator is also one of the characters in the scene, and he/she tells the story using the words "I," "me," etc.

A narrative is told from a particular point of view. The point of view refers to the angle of vision—the point from which the people, events and other details in a story are viewed and told. A narrative essay is generally written in the first person, which is, using "I." A first-person narrative produces a personal relationship with the reader, which tends to be more subjective. While a third-person narrative may sound more objective by deliberately refraining the writer from entering the minds of any of his/her characters and tells a story as though it were a play taking place before his/her eyes. The narrator speaks as "he," "she," "they" or by name.

3.1.1 How to write short stories in the first person

There are certain things a first person narrator normally shouldn't say. For example: "My bald spot looked particularly shiny that day." Why? Because you can't see your own bald spot unless you're looking at yourself in a photograph or a mirror at just the right angle.

Another thing that sounds strange in the first person voice is, "I have no idea that..." Your first person narrator can't give information he doesn't know. If your narrator has been locked in the trunk of a car, it will be hard for him to describe what the police are doing just then to solve his kidnapping.

Also always an awkward statement is, "Then, I died."

Therefore, first-person narration has its limitations such as limited scope and limited voice.

— Limited scope—Your narrator only knows what he/she knows. He/she doesn't know what the other people around him/her are thinking. He/she doesn't know what's happening two miles away. That limits the information he/she can supply to the reader.

— Limited voice—If your narrator is a seven-year-old, he/she can't talk convincingly about politics. One thing that drives the readers crazy is when a first-person narrator who is supposed to be a child, or an uneducated farm worker or manual laborer suddenly launches into a poetic description of the weather using twenty-dollar words and references to Greek philosophers.

3.1.2 How to write short stories in the third person

Third-person narrators may also have limited or complete access to one or more character's thoughts. It is common to locate the narrator partially inside a particular character's head.

e.g.

Jack felt faint as he hurried out of the bank, wondering if the police were already outside. What would happen to Miriam if he were arrested? The thought was unbearable; he tried to push it out of his mind.

The effect here is almost as if this had been written in the first person, with Jack telling the story.

But with a third-person narrator, the writer is not limited by Jack's voice. He/she might choose to limit his/her third-person narrator to Jack's perspective. This would give readers a sense of connection to Jack, as if they were living his particular experience. Or the writer could move from one character's mind to another. If you switch points of view in the same story, you have to be careful not to confuse or disorient your reader. You might decide to limit yourself to one viewpoint for each section of the story and use line breaks or another visual cue to let your reader know when you're switching.

Ex. 3-1-1 *Read the following essay and find out which person the writer uses.*

English Is Confusing

"Good evening, everybody!" said the teacher, Donna. "Where is everybody?" That was sort of a daily joke by Donna. Usually the class started with only two or three students present, and then filled up as the minutes went by. It was summertime. Summer school was only eight weeks long. Class attendance was always smaller than during fall and spring semesters.

"I don't know, teacher. Maybe they late or no come," said one student. "Maybe watching TV football tonight."

"Is there a soccer game tonight? It seems like there's a soccer game every night. Oh, well. Let's get started, okay? We're on page 36 in the workbook. Tonight we're studying participles as adjectives. Students are always confused when they learn about the present and past participles, so we will practice this a lot. Tonight, we're just going to practice the present participle.

"The present participle tells us what emotion or feeling the subject is causing. For example, 'Grammar is boring' means that the subject 'grammar' causes an emotion of boredom. If we say, 'The movie is interesting,' we are saying that the movie causes a feeling of interest. If we say, 'The roller coaster is exciting,' we are saying that the roller coaster causes a feeling of excitement. Any questions so far? Am I confusing you? Is everyone confused?"

The classroom was quiet. Donna looked at blank faces. They were confused. She knew this would take a while. But eventually, the faster students would grasp it, and then they would help the slower students. By the end of the evening, most of the class would feel comfortable using the present participle.

Donna erased the board and put some new examples on it. She loved guiding her students through difficult topics like this one. She always felt a little bit thrilled when the look of understanding came to their faces.

3.2 Thesis Statement

A narrative makes and supports a point. That is the purpose in telling a story. In writing a narrative of some incident you have experienced, it is likely that you have some definite points to make. You may want to prove a theory, to illustrate a concept, to praise a virtue, to condemn a vice, etc. That point is called your **thesis**—your opinion about your topic. In most cases, your topic is the incident you are telling the story of, and your opinion is what the incident taught you.

Ex.3-2-1 *Question: What is the purpose of the essay?*

The Road to Adulthood

Like most little girls, I thought it would be very grown up to get my hair done in a beauty parlor instead of by my mother or older sister as it had been done for years. I also knew that at a beauty parlor I would get my limp dull hair changed into shining curls, and I wanted curls more than anything. I was positive that blond waves were just what I needed to acquire the maturity of popularity so essential in the third grade.

For a month, I cried and badgered my family, promising everything if they would only let me get my hair done as I wished. Finally, after hearing enough of my whining, my mother gave in and made an appointment for me. I was sure I was on my way to becoming an adorable Shirley Temple.

Things didn't turn out quite the way I imagined. To begin with, I was not taken to one of the fashionable beauty houses I had often seen on my way home from school, but rather to the oldest salon in town. Its outdated interior hosted only a few older women getting their thin hair inexpertly teased over their visibly pink scalps. I should have suspected then and there that things would not be the way I dreamed, but still, naïve, I waited for my transformation. I sat through my appointment nutmeat, never questioning the mass of hair that fell to the floor, nor the burning sensation as the rollers were pulled tight against my head. In fact, it wasn't until I arrived home that I was able to take a good look in the mirror to see what had happened. Looking back at me was not a reflection of a cute, curly top, but instead, a mop of indescribable frizz: the classic example of the overworked permanent.

Needless to say, I overreacted and spent the remaining part of the day washing and re-washing my hair to remove the tangled mess. When this did little to improve the situation, I cried hysterically for hours, my head well hidden beneath a pillow. It took a week until I would see anyone without a towel over my head, and a month before I could look at someone without feeling that they were making fun of me the minute I turned my back.

When I think about how silly I behaved, I always laugh. Now it seems easy to accept such small disappointment, but if you had asked me then I would have assured you that nothing could possibly have been worse. In a way, I feel that such a fruitless journey to the hairdresser actually helped me a bit further along the road to adulthood, since it was a perfect example of a disappointing obstacle that can be improved only by time and patience, and not by tantrums or senseless worrying.

3.3 Organization

A narrative involves a careful organization. The event is usually presented in chronological order, that is, in the order they occur. Occasionally, flashbacks (starting from the middle or even the end of the story and then going back to the beginning) are used to arouse the reader's interest. A typical three-part format of a narrative consists of an introduction, a main body and a conclusion. The introduction presents the topic and thesis as well as the context of the story. The main body explains and supports that thesis by focusing on key aspects of the topic, and the conclusion functions to remind the reader of what the main point was.

Ex.3-3-1 *Discuss the following questions.*
1. What is the purpose of the story?
2. Are the *who*, *where* and *when* made clear in the narrative?
3. Elaborate the structure of the story, that is, the beginning, the middle and the end.
4. How are the paragraphs linked?

Take Me Out to the Ball Game

Ralph and Ilene hadn't been to a baseball game in about five years. They were only 15 miles from the stadium, but the heavy traffic on game day made those 15 miles seem more like 60 miles. It took about an hour to get to the stadium. Then, when the game was over, it took half an hour just to get out of the parking lot. Then the drive home was another hour. In other words, the traveling took longer than the game itself.

"Honey, the Giants are in town," Ilene said. "I want to see Barry Bonds hit a home run. Can we go to the game? We haven't gone in such a long time."

"You're right. It has been a while. OK, I'll go if you don't mind driving," said Ralph.

"Great! Let's get ready. If we get there early enough, I might get his autograph. Maybe he'll hit a foul ball we can catch." Ilene was excited. "We!?" Ralph thought.

An hour later they were in their car. They lived in Pasadena near an old church. They went south on Orange Grove and then south on the 110 freeway. The 110 is California's original freeway, full of twists and turns. Accidents occur daily; Californian drivers think yellow lights and sharp curves mean the same thing—speed up!

The traffic was lighter than they expected. They arrived at the stadium 40 minutes before game time. They paid the $8 parking fee, parked and locked the car, and walked to the main entrance.

Several individuals were standing around outside the stadium, looking casual but actually selling tickets on the sly. "Are you going to buy from a scalper?" asked Ilene.

"Yes. Just like last time. That one looks honest," Ralph replied.

They walked over to a man in a red cap. Ralph's instincts were correct. The man had tickets for good seats at a fair price. Ralph gave the man $45 and thanked him.

"Don't thank me, my friend. Thank your local police department. Put your hands behind your back, please. You're under arrest."

"What?" Ralph was astonished. "What's going on?"

"Buying scalped tickets is illegal in Los Angeles," said the undercover police officer. "It's been illegal for 25 years. Don't worry. The police station is right outside the park. We'll have you back here right after we book you. You can pay the $150 fine with your credit card." The officer handcuffed Ralph.

"This has got to be a joke. You people have never enforced this law before," said Ralph.

"Well, we've got a new mayor and he wants us to enforce all the laws that bring in money. Come with me, please. I'll have you back here in 20 minutes. Ma'am, you can wait here for him. You might want to buy some legitimate tickets while you're waiting. Have a nice day. Oh, and enjoy the game!"

3.4 Supporting Details

A narrative relies on concrete details to support and convey its point. All of the details relate to the main point the writer is attempting to make. Therefore, details should be carefully selected to create a unified, forceful effect and a dominant impression. In the presentation of details, verbs and modifiers are usually vivid and precise. Dialogues may also be employed.

Ex.3-4-1 *Discuss the following questions.*

1. What is the purpose of the essay?
2. Are the *who*, *where* and *when* made clear in the narrative?
3. List relevant details selected by the writer to bring out his main ideas.

The Fun They Had

Margie even wrote about it that night in her diary. On the page headed May 17, 2157, she wrote, "Today, Tommy found a real book!"

It was a very old book. Margie's grandfather once said that when he was a little boy his grandfather told him that there was a time when all stories were printed on paper.

They turned the pages, which were yellow and crinkly, and it was awfully funny to read words that stood still instead of moving the way they were supposed to—on a screen, you know. And then, when they turned back to the page before, it had the same words on it that it had had when they read it the first time.

"Gee," said Tommy, "what a waste. When you're through with the book, you just throw it away, I guess. Our television screen must have had a million books on it and it's good for plenty more. I *wouldn't throw it away."*

"Same with mine," said Margie. She was eleven and hadn't seen as many telebooks as Tommy had. He was thirteen. She said, "Where did you find it?"

"In my house." He pointed without looking, because he was busy reading. "In the attic." "What's it about?" "School."

Margie was scornful. "School? What's there to write about school? I hate school."

Margie always hated school, but now she hated it more than ever. The mechanical teacher had been giving her test after test in geography and she had been doing worse and worse until her mother had shaken her head sorrowfully and sent for the County Inspector.

He was a round little man with a red face and a whole box of tools with dials and wires. He smiled at Margie and gave her an apple, then took the teacher apart. Margie had hoped he wouldn't know how to put it together again, but he knew how all right, and, after an hour or so, there it was again, large and black and ugly, with a big screen on which all the lessons were shown and the questions were asked. That wasn't so bad. The part Margie hated most was the slot where she had to put homework and test papers. She always had to write them out in a punch code they made her learn when she was six years old, and the mechanical teacher calculated the mark in no time.

The Inspector had smiled after he was finished and patted Margie's head. He said to her mother, "It's not the little girl's fault, Mrs. Jones. I think the geography sector was geared a little too quick. Those things happen sometimes. I've slowed it up to an average ten-year level. Actually, the over-all pattern of her progress is quite satisfactory." And he patted Margie's head again.

Margie was disappointed. She had been hoping they would take the teacher away altogether. They had once taken Tommy's teacher away for nearly a month because the history sector had blanked out completely.

So she said to Tommy, "Why would anyone write about school?"

Tommy looked at her with very superior eyes. "Because it's not our kind of school, stupid. This is the old kind of school that they had hundreds and hundreds of years ago." He added loftily, pronouncing the word carefully, "**Centuries** ago."

Margie was hurt. "Well, I don't know what kind of school they had all that time ago." She read the book over his shoulder for a while, then said, "Anyway, they had a teacher."

"Sure they had a teacher, but it wasn't a regular teacher. It was a man." "A man? How could a man be a teacher?" "Well, he just told the boys and girls things and gave them homework and asked them questions." "A man isn't smart enough." "Sure he is. My father knows as much as my teacher." "He can't. A man can't know as much as a teacher." "He knows almost as much, I bet cha."

Margie wasn't prepared to dispute that. She said, "I wouldn't want a strange man in my house to teach me."

Tommy screamed with laughter. "You don't know much, Margie. The teachers didn't live in the house. They had a special building and all the kids went there." "And all the kids learned the same thing?" "Sure, if they were the same age."

"But my mother says a teacher has to be adjusted to fit the mind of each boy and girl it teaches and that each kid has to be taught differently."

"Just the same they didn't do it that way then. If you don't like it, you don't have to read the book."

"I didn't say I didn't like it," Margie said quickly. She wanted to read about those funny schools.

They weren't even half-finished when Margie's mother called, "Margie! School!" Margie looked up. "Not yet, Mamma."

"Now!" said Mrs. Jones. "And it's probably time for Tommy, too."

Margie said to Tommy, "Can I read the book some more with you after school?"

"Maybe," he said nonchalantly. He walked away whistling, the dusty old book tucked beneath his arm.

Margie went into the schoolroom. It was right next to her bedroom, and the mechanical teacher was on and waiting for her. It was always on at the same time every day except Saturday and Sunday, because her mother said little girls learned better if they learned at regular hours.

The screen was lit up, and it said: "Today's arithmetic lesson is on the addition of proper fractions. Please insert yesterday's homework in the proper slot."

Margie did so with a sigh. She was thinking about the old schools they had when her grandfather's grandfather was a little boy. All the kids from the whole neighborhood came, laughing and shouting in the schoolyard, sitting together in the schoolroom, going home together at the end of the day. They learned the same things, so they could help one another on the homework and talk about it.

And the teachers were people...

The mechanical teacher was flashing on the screen: "When we add the fractions 1/2 and 1/4..."

Margie was thinking about how the kids must have loved it in the old days. She was thinking about the fun they had.

Suggested topics for narrative essays

1. A childhood event. Think of an experience when you learned something for the first time, or when you realized how important someone was for you.

2. Achieving a goal. Think about a particularly meaningful achievement in your life. This could be something as seemingly minor as achieving a good grade on a difficult assignment, or this could be something with more long-lasting effects, like getting the job you desired or getting into the best school to which you applied.

3. A failure. Think about a time when you did not perform as well as you had wanted. Focusing on an experience like this can result in rewarding reflections about the positive emerging from the negative.

4. A good or bad deed. Think about a time when you did or did not stand up for yourself or someone else in the face of adversity or challenge.

5. A change in your life. Think about a time when something significant changed your life. This could be anything from a move across town to a major change in a relationship to the birth or death of a loved one.

6. A realization. Think about a time when you experienced a realization. This could be anything from understanding a complicated math equation to gaining a deeper understanding of a philosophical issue or life situation.

Thinking critically about narration

1. Think about your story and about what you want to say to your readers in your narration.

2. Ask what experience or series of events you want to write about and why.

3. What is important about this story? What was important to you about what happened?

4. What main point do you want to make about this story?

5. To convey the main point, what events do you need to tell about? What details, examples and facts will bring the event to life to the readers?

6. Do you want to report anything that was said?

7. Would the use of time transitions help the readers follow the sequence of the events more easily?

8. Make a plan and then write a clear, strong and convincing narration that gets the main point across to the readers.

Chapter Four
Description

Introduction

Description is a mode of writing which is relied upon in other modes, so we sometimes find difficulty in imagining a purely descriptive essay. For example, narration can involve description, but narration is more concerned with what happened than with what things look like. In a narrative essay, description can make the setting of characters more vivid. Narration asks the writer to put events and actions in a certain order or sequence, while description does not have to follow any chronological sequence. It emphasizes our sensory impressions instead. That is, we can put down in an essay of descriptive writing what we see, hear, touch, smell and taste. In a word, description aims at presenting pictures in words of people, places, objects, scenes, moments or events. The purpose of a purely descriptive essay is to involve the reader enough so that he/she can actually visualize the things being described.

Some conventions of descriptive essays

- A descriptive essay can be objective or subjective, giving the writer a wide choice of tone, diction and attitude. For instance, an objective description of one's dog would mention such facts as height, weight, coloring, and so forth. A subjective description would include not only the above details, but would also stress the writer's feeling toward the dog, as well as its personality and habits.
- A descriptive essay has one, clear dominant impression. If, for example, you are describing a snowfall, it is important for you to decide and to let your reader know if it is threatening or lovely; in order to have one dominant impression, it cannot be both. The dominant impression guides the writer's selection of detail and is thereby made clear to the reader in the thesis sentence.
- In a descriptive essay, the writer must carefully select specific and concrete details, from which the dominant impression is built. Be sure that the details are consistent with the dominant impression. In other words, the writer has the license to omit details which are incongruent with the

dominant impression.

- A typical three-part descriptive essay involves the following organization: the first paragraph gives an introduction, describing the general feel of the place, person or thing. The body paragraphs offer in-depth descriptions of two or three particular aspects of the place, person or thing. In the last paragraph, the writer steps out of the descriptive mode and offers a brief conclusion of what the place, person or thing says about him/her.

Ex.4-1 *Find the adjectives and adverbs in this paragraph and underline them. Pay attention to the verbs showing how Helen felt the things around.*

I feel the delicate symmetry of a leaf. I pass my hands lovingly about the smooth skin of a silver birch, or the rough bark of a pine. In spring I touch the branches of trees hopefully in search of a bud, the first sign of awakening Nature after her winter's sleep. I feel the delightful texture of a flower, and discover its remarkable folds; and something of the miracle of Nature is revealed to me. Occasionally, if I am very fortunate, I place my hand gently in a small tree and feel the happy quiver of a bird in full song. I am delighted to have cool water of a brook rush through my open fingers. To me, a thick carpet of pine needles or soft grass is more welcome than the most luxurious Persian rug. To me, the colorful seasons are a thrilling and unending drama, the action of which streams through my finger tips.

Ex.4-2 *Discussion questions.*
1. What is the pattern of organization in the following passage?
2. What is the central focus of the description?
3. What relevant details does the writer choose?
4. How many kinds of sensory details does the writer use?
5. Are there any precise words that leave you deep impression? And what are they?
6. What kinds of figurative language are used by the writer? Underline the sentences.

Our Campus

There is a very beautiful garden on campus. As you enter the garden through the university gate, you will find an elegant pavilion standing right in the center. At the back of the pavilion are some white stone benches. Both the pavilion and the benches add more charm to the fantastic scenery. To the left of the pavilion is the woods with all kinds of trees. When you sit on the benches or stand under the pavilion, you can listen to the birds singing in the woods and the trees talking with the wind gently. To the right, there is a flower bed with hundreds of flowers in full bloom. Here, the sight and the fragrance are the most intoxicating. Then don't forget the lawns on both sides of the gate. The lawn on the right attracts particular attention due to a lovely pond in its center, where a school of red and black carps are swimming leisurely and the water is shining in the sun. I love the garden and I love our campus.

Ex. 4-3 *Discussion questions.*

1. What is the pattern of organization of the following passage?
2. What is the central focus of the description?
3. What relevant details does the writer choose?
4. How many kinds of sensory details does the writer use?
5. Are there any precise vocabularies that leave you deep impression? And what are they?
6. What kinds of figurative language are used by the writer? Underline the sentences.

My Own Little World

The door to my study is nearly always closed. It's the place I go to read and work in tranquility. Today, however, I'm inviting you in for a visit.

As you open the door, notice the Guatemalan crucifix with its bright gold and maroon flowers; it joyfully reminds me to dedicate my work to God. Although the room is small, I hope you find it cozy. A big cheerful window lets in the morning sunshine, which saturates the room with its warmth and embraces us with light. Birds chirp outside, beckoning you to enter.

An old-fashioned doctor's desk with brass drawer handles sits in front of the window, its wood full of nicks from many careless moves and tow. May I introduce you to Ralph, my friendly computer, who sits on top of the desk? When I turn him on, he'll crackle "hello" and blink an inviting amber command on the screen. That's my dog Chico under the desk, snoring in harmony with Ralph and the birds.

Against the left wall are my book cases, sagging with the wise weight of cheap paperbacks and a few expensive gold-spined volumes interspersed. A bronzed Indian chief in a watercolor squints knowingly at us from the wall. Won't you have a seat in the tattered old green armchair nestled in the other corner? I know you smell the freshly perked coffee. I made it specially for your visit. Use my favorite cup there on the tray; it's the one with red and blue balloons around the rim.

Stay as long as you wish, but when you're ready to leave, be sure to close the door behind you. I like the peaceful security of this, my own little world.

Suggested topics for descriptive essays

Write a descriptive composition using the five senses. You can use one or two of them, or all of them.

1. Our campus in early spring.
2. The most important holidays that you celebrate.

Chapter Five
Exposition

Introduction

Expository writing is the type of writing that most of us encounter in our daily lives. It can be seen in papers that describe a process or event or how to do something; articles that analyze events, ideas or objects and research reports both at school or work. "With its emphasis on 'logic' and 'organization,' expository writing is most likely the type of writing you will be doing in college and throughout your career. …your ability to write exposition requires the same skills necessary to succeed in many careers: thinking critically, analyzing complex situations, and presenting information clearly to coworkers." (Luis, Deborah & William Lewis, *Bridges to Better Writing*. Wadsworth, 2010). In essence, expository writing or exposition is simply a writing that expresses an idea and backs it up with facts. It is used to describe, explain, define or otherwise inform a reader about a specific subject.

Though one of the most clear-cut of the four types of writing, expository writing may be one of the most difficult to learn because it may include elements of narration, description and argumentation. But always keep in mind that exposition is about conveying information and the primary goal is to present, completely and fairly, other people's views or to report about an event or a situation.

Some conventions of expository essays
- **Organization**

An expository essay has the same basic structure as any essay. A typical three-part expository essay involves the following organization: introduction, body and conclusion.

(1) In the introductory paragraph, the thesis statement is defined and narrowed down until it becomes narrow enough to be supported within the entire essay.

(2) Each body paragraph has a distinct controlling topic giving an overview of the main point of the paragraph. Then the evidence and the writer's analysis based on the evidence can be presented.

The use of transitional words or phrases can help the reader follow along and reinforce the logic. The paragraph ends with a conclusion sentence that also serves as a transition to the next paragraph.

(3) The conclusion paragraph provides a brief summary of the overall argument made throughout the essay. It restates the thesis and the main supporting ideas (though the sentences should be worded differently) and hopefully, reinforces the writer's position in a meaningful and memorable way.

- **Language features**

(1) Expositions are simply essays that explain something with facts, as opposed to opinion. So it should be devoid of the writer's criticism and personal opinions or unnecessary descriptive language.

(2) Clarity is essential in expository writing. If the essay cannot be understood, it is of no value. So always choose simple and exact words or expressions and avoid ornamental or ambiguous words. Besides, try to use action verbs and minimize the use of linking verbs.

(3) Since expository writing is factual and is written without emotion, it is better to stay away from first and second person pronouns. For example, in an expository essay about how to make chocolate chip cookies, the following thesis statement, "I really like chocolate chip cookies and I will tell you how to make them," is unfocused. The subject of the sentence is "I" rather than "chocolate chip cookies." The focus, then, is lost by placing emphasis on the writer rather than the reader. The thesis can be rephrased as "Chocolate chip cookies are a delicious treat and can be made in five easy steps."

Types of expository essays and methods to develop an essay

1. An expository essay attempts to explain the subject to the readers. It is writing that makes matters clear, or offers insights or otherwise casts light on a subject. This may be accomplished by presenting facts and statistical information, explaining a process, discussing the similarities and differences between two items, identifying a cause-effect relationship, analyzing problems and solutions, explaining with examples, dividing and classifying, or defining.

2. Depending upon the particular type of expository essay being written and the writer's purpose, one pattern or method or a combination of them can be employed to create an exposition. The frequently used methods include definition with explanation and exemplification, process, classification, cause-effect, problem-solution, comparison and so on. The sequence of presentation of supporting details may vary. The process essay may employ chronological order, while the essay which compares or contrasts, explains with examples, or divides and classifies may use an order of importance (most-to-least important or least-to-most important). The essay which employs causal analysis may identify a cause and then predict its effect or start with the effect and seek to identify its cause.

5.1 Expository Essay of Definition

In academic writing, definition paragraphs are frequently required to explain concept or words or to make them clearer to a reader. They should be supported by facts, examples or personal experience to fully explain the defined.

Useful expressions:

A means ...; The meaning of A is...; A is ...; A refers to ...; A can be defined as...

A definition paragraph explains the meaning and significance of something. The topic sentence gives three pieces of information: the topic, the large category or group and the distinguishing characteristics. It can also take the form of an appositive or an adjective clause.

Sample 5-1-1

Wisdom

Wisdom is a personality possession that one gains over a lifetime of experience. It is a possession that is bestowed upon a person, rather than one that the person recognizes on his or her own. Wisdom incorporates many other traits, but the requirement that it is recognized by people other than the ones possessing it sets wisdom apart from other personality traits. Wisdom is a compilation of a life's experience marked by humility, kairos and unselfishness.

Wisdom is an idea that is often confused with or improperly attributed to old age. Not all old people are wise, though many are. Conversely, not all wise people are old. One often hears the phrase "wise beyond years" in reference to a young person who displays the traits of wisdom. However, true wisdom is a result of strong life experiences. Naturally, older folks have had more experiences from which to draw wisdom, so it is easy to limit wisdom to old people. But, the key to wisdom is the strength of the experience. A young person may have an extraordinary experience which teaches him or her a powerful lesson. Lessons of this type often transform into wisdom.

Experience is just one of the major ingredients of wisdom; humility is also a requirement. Because wisdom is bestowed upon a person by virtue of others' recognition, humility must be a possession of the wise person. To claim wisdom for oneself is foolishness. Humility is characterized by a person's unwillingness to be the center of attention or by a person's quickness to share credit or place others in a superior position. One who is wise recognizes that the standing of others should take precedence to his or her own standing. Therefore, the wise person takes in account what is best for others when offering advice or information.

In addition to experience and humility, wisdom also incorporates the Greek term kairos. Kairos means proper timing and measure in all things. A wise person does not offer more than is required, nor does he or she omit relevant information. The mark of true wisdom is also a sense of timing that is most beneficial to the inquirer. As with humility, a wise person does not take in account what will be most timely for himself or herself, but what is best for the other person. The wise person knows when to step into a situation and when to let things run their courses. The wise person has the ability to understand not only a situation, but the people within that situation. The last mark of wisdom is unselfishness. Unselfishness differs from humility in the respect that humility requires someone to be praised or recognized in order to deflect that praise or recognition onto others. Unselfishness requires nothing more than the constant thought of others' interests and wellbeing over ones' own. This mark of wisdom sets true wisdom apart from mere intelligence or learning. Anyone can have the right answer at the right time, but only those who possess true wisdom are ready to sacrifice themselves and their own interests to provide sound advice or information to others. This is the essential part of unselfishness as it marks wisdom.

True wisdom requires all three qualities: humility, kairos and unselfishness. The experienced person who has one or two of the three qualities, but not all of the three, cannot be truly wise. The experienced person who possesses all the three traits must also have these qualities recognized by others, rather than recognize and claim the traits for himself or herself. Only the possession of experience, humility, kairos, unselfishness and the recognition of others makes a truly wise person.

Sample 5-1-2

What Is Mathematics?

This may sound as a trivial question, but the answer is much more complex than that, so every study of mathematics should begin with defining what, in fact, it is.

The very word "mathematics" is of a Greek origin and it is very symbolic, for it was in ancient Greece where it got its more or less modern meaning. The word from which it originates means simply "science" or "learning," but already in ancient times it has developed and expanded towards its modern meaning.

Mathematics is one of the purely abstract sciences, for it studies numbers, quantities, changes, structures, patterns—the things that exist only as far as there are people to perceive them and created only by people's abstractions. Even among the mathematicians themselves there is no unanimity about whether the concepts they study actually exist. Nevertheless, mathematics as a science developed from primitive activities like counting or measurement, observations of objects in reality and so on, and only in course of time moved into the sphere of pure abstraction.

Logic, or mathematical rigor, is one of the most notable features of mathematics. In short, it means that any research in this science is susceptible to proof checking that may with 100% confidence state whether it is right or wrong. Although this idea already existed in antiquity, it was a kind of unattainable ideal until the beginning of the 20th century, when calculating machines made it possible to actually proof-check almost any mathematical construction.

Despite its abstract nature, throughout history mathematics has been used in application to objective reality in many spheres of human activity, from architecture to warfare, thus giving birth to the field of applied mathematics of contemporary times. Although in the minds of many mathematicians there remains something far-away and unattainable, even the pure mathematical *studies often lead to discoveries that find way into our everyday life. In some curious sense, mathematics, while studying the subject matter that does not correspond to any physical reality, serves as a medium between almost all the other sciences, for many problems that arise from them find the realization of their solution in mathematics and nowhere else.*

5.2   Expository Essay of Process

The process paragraphs explain how to do or make something. Describing a process (how to do an experiment in a laboratory report or how to apply for a university admission, etc.) is an essential academic skill. Process paragraphs are usually organized chronologically, so that the readers can follow closely the process being described. Therefore, precision in diction and logic progression from one step to another are necessary for successful process writing.

Useful expressions:

first, (second, etc.) then; now; next; finally; after that; meanwhile; the first step; the next step; after five minutes; as soon as; before; until; whenever

Sample 5-2-1

How to Build a One-Match Campfire

Building a campfire that you can light with one match is simple if you follow these easy steps. The first step is to prepare a safe place for your campfire. Clear an area on the ground at least 3 feet wide, and put a circle of stones around it. Second, gather fuel. You will need several sizes of fuel: small twigs, medium sticks and large sticks. The next step is to build a tepee. Put a handful of twigs in a small pile and use the small sticks to build a small tepee over the pile. Leave spaces large enough to drop a lighted match through. Next, build a cabin around the tepee using the medium sticks. Fifth, place two large pieces of wood on either side of the cabin, and lay two or three long sticks on top to make a loose roof. The last step is to light a match and drop it through a space in the tepee. Soon you will enjoy the warmth of a nice fire, and your friends will admire your skill at lighting a campfire with only one match!

5.3   Expository Essay of Classification/Division

Classification is a pattern used to divide or categorize subjects into distinct groups based on some common basis. A single subject can be classified in various ways, according to different "classes." For example, words may fall into the basic word stock and non-basic vocabulary by word frequency, into content words and functional words by notion, and into native words and borrowed words by origin. Therefore, throughout the essay, one single classification principle should be adhered to consistently. Make sure that the classes do not overlap.

> **Useful expressions:**
>
> *A can be divided into…;*
> *There are 3 kinds of …;*
> *A comes into 2 varieties.*
> *A may fall into 3 categories.*
> *A can be classified into… ;*
> *according to/on the basis of /depending on…*

Sample 5-3-1

Cybercriminals

"*Cybercriminals generally fall into one of the three categories,*" he (Michael DeCesare, president of McAfee) says. *First, there are the "Anonymouses of the world" or the hacktivists—people who expose information about a company or government they morally oppose. Second, the organized crime. "They're realizing there's far more money in cybercrime than prostitution,"* Mr. DeCesare says. "*You can buy somebody's I.D. for less than $10 online.*" *Third, the activities funded by states and other political groups.* "*Every government has a cyber division,*" he says, *including the U.S. But cyber dangers now stretch beyond state lines to groups such as al Qaeda.* "*Cybercrime is a lot like that—[the country is] almost not relevant anymore, making it difficult to hold governments accountable.*"

Sample 5-3-2

Types of Computers

There are a lot of terms used to describe computers. Most of these words imply the size, expected use or capability of the computer. While the term "computer" can apply to virtually any device that has a microprocessor in it, most people think of a computer as a device that receives input from the user through a mouse or keyboard, processes it in some fashion and displays the result on a screen. Computers can be divided into five types according to the purposes they are used for and their capabilities.

The most familiar type of microprocessor is the personal computer (PC). It is designed for general use by a single person. While a Mac is also a PC, most people relate the term with systems that run the Windows operating system. PCs were first known as microcomputers because they were a complete computer but built on a smaller scale than the huge systems in use by most businesses. A PC can come in two types [three if we include the Personal Digital Assistants (PDAs) that differ from PCs not by the working policy but in appearance as well.]: desktop and laptop. The former is not designed for portability. The expectation with desktop systems is that you will set the computer up in a permanent location. Most desktops offer more power, storage and versatility for less cost than their portable brethren. On the other hand, the laptops—also called notebooks—are portable computers that integrate the display, keyboard, a pointing device or trackball, processor, memory and hard drive all in a battery-operated package, slightly larger than an average hardcover book.

Another purpose for using a microprocessor is as a workstation. The computers used for this purpose have a more powerful processor, additional memory and enhanced capabilities for performing a special group of tasks, such as 3D Graphics or game development.

A computer can also be used as a server. For this, it needs to be optimized to provide services to other computers over a network. Servers usually have powerful processors, lots of memory and large hard drives.

A fourth type, a main frame is the heart of a network of computers or terminals which allows hundreds of people to work at the same time on the same data. It is indispensable for the business world.

Sometimes, computers can be used for specialized fields as well. The supercomputer is the top of the heap in power and expense. It is used for jobs that take massive amounts of calculating, like weather forecasting, engineering design and testing, serious decryption, and economic forecasting.

With the increasing demand in different specialties, new adjustments are being made to microprocessors and new types of computers that serve different purposes emerge. In this ongoing process, it would not be possible to put a full stop here. What we suggest is that it is better to keep an eye on the development of science in this field and keep updating our knowledge in order not to be out-of-date like the computers of old times that were as big as a room.

Sample 5-3-3

Physics

In the course of time, physics as a science underwent great changes. From a subdivision of philosophy, it gradually turned into an applied science and then, in the 20th century, into an extremely complicated, greatly specialized and somewhat closed science. For the majority of this time, physics has been rather ambiguously limited, describing the movements of celestial bodies and other material objects that stand behind the construction of many mechanisms and so on. To be a physicist was to know something about all these fields. But in the 20th century and, especially after the works of Albert Einstein, everything changed. Physics split into a number of very narrow and very specialized fields, sometimes with little connection between each other. The majority of scientists work in one and the same field their entire lives.

The most important modern spheres of physics are as follows:

(1) Atomic, molecular and optical (AMO) physics deals with interactions between light and matter at a scale of single atom or construction consisting of only several atoms. They approach their subject matter both from the point of view of quantum and classical attitude and generally tend to study things on a microscopic level.

(2) Condensed matter physics, on the contrary, deals with matter and its properties on a macroscopic level. Nowadays it is the largest and most well-developed field of physics, and no wonder—in fact, for the most of its existence physics was constituted primarily by these studies. The modern condensed matter physics has evolved from solid-state physics, which in turn became one of its subfields.

(3) Particle or high energy physics studies the properties of elementary components of energy and matter. Very often it studies phenomena that do not exist naturally, but can only be created artificially by means of causing different elementary particles to collide. This field of physics was recently made a part of popular culture due to the scandal concerning the Big Hadron Collider and the end of the world it was supposed to cause.

The rest is interdisciplinary sciences, such as astrophysics, geophysics and biophysics. They study the physical properties of subject matters belonging to other natural sciences. There are a number of less orthodox connections, but they are less well-formed.

5.4 Expository Essay of Cause-and-effect

Cause-effect essays investigate why things are as they are, or why something happened, or the effects of an event or a situation. Causes and effects can occur either in the same paragraph or separately. A cause paragraph usually answers the question "Why." It usually begins with the effect and then explains the causes of the effect. An effect paragraph often answers the question "What." It usually begins with a topic sentence that describes the event or a result.

Useful expressions:

A may lead to/result in/give rise to/cause B.
B results from/stems from/is caused by A.
therefore; consequently; as a result (of); thus; because (of); due to; since; for this reason

Sample 5-4-1

How Social Media Affects Family Relationships

A family has, at most times, been a private territory. No matter what happened outside of it, for example at work or elsewhere, a family, in principle, is where many people can share their problems, seek for solutions together and enjoy understanding and privacy. However, as technologies have become more and more advanced, this private, intimate space has shrunk. Today, in the era of social media, relationships in many families have changed, since social media affects these relationships in a number of unexpected and sometimes negative ways.

Looking from an optimistic perspective, children and parents have gained a powerful tool of communication. Indeed, while communicating in person might be difficult for both teenagers and their parents during the so-called "teenage rioting" period, social networks provide a valuable opportunity for communication. However, there is another side of the coin. About 30% of people are now using all kinds of gadgets, including cell phones, tablets, and so on, to talk to their loved ones through social media services, instead of having a conversation with them in person. One person out of five admitted they learned what their family members were doing by checking their statuses online, not by asking them personally—even though they might be sitting in the next room.

Moreover, a study on media influence done by the Kaiser Family Foundation shows that young people from the age of 8 to 18 years old tend to spend about seven hours a day using entertainment media, which makes a total of approximately 50 hours per week. It means that during this time they are not exercising, hanging out, communicating with their families, or getting involved in intimate relationships. Such a lifestyle makes them gain extra weight, get easily distracted, and develop difficulties in establishing interpersonal relationships, including the relationships with parents, siblings and other family members. The study suggests that such young people often tend to be mentally absent when being with a group of friends or family (Huffington Post).

Yet another problem originating from social media is the real lack of privacy within families. When there is a conflict, fight, regular problem or even some happy event, one (and sometimes both) of the spouses occasionally post about it on Facebook or share this information with the public in some other way. This leads to a transparency of relationships, and thus its vulnerability; also, one of the spouses might be frustrated by the fact that intimate details of their family life are being exposed to a large number of unfamiliar people. This leads to additional conflicts, further posting about these conflicts in social media and thus creates an endless circle of problems (IFR).

Social media possesses many useful features, but in the case of family relationships, these media services should be used with caution. According to different studies, teenagers widely using social media tend to communicate with their family members in person much less often. They may face difficulties connected to social adaptation and acceptance, as well as excessive body weight and communication problems. Also, social media may be used by family members to share the intimate details of family life with public; this can be frustrating for family members.

Sample 5-4-2

Obesity

Obesity has become a major problem in the UAE. Over 60% of Emirati nationals are overweight. This is a difficult problem with many serious effects on the individual and country.

Obesity can be divided into three main causes—diet, lifestyle and education. One of the chief causes is diet. Young Emiratis eat more and more high-carbohydrate, high-fat burgers and pizza in fast-food restaurants. However, some traditional foods are also very oily, and because of increasing affluence they are eaten more often than in the past. Lifestyle is a second main cause of obesity. As a result of cheap foreign labour, many Emiratis now have sedentary jobs and do not exercise regularly.

However, one of the main causes is lack of education and awareness. The society's attitude to food often leads to over-consumption. Parents do not teach good eating habits to children, and many people lack knowledge about good nutrition or a balanced diet.

Obesity affects the individual and the country. The biggest effect is on the individual. First of all, being overweight has health risks. Obesity can lead to heart disease, diabetes and other conditions. The quality of life suffers, as it is difficult to enjoy exercise or move. Another result is lack of self-esteem. This can lead to depression, eating disorders and crash diets. The country is also affected. It becomes very expensive for the government to provide advanced medical care such as heart transplants. Unhealthy citizens are also less productive.

Obesity or even being overweight has serious effects on the individual and the society. Both need to take action to examine the causes of this problem and find solutions.

5.5 Expository Essay of Problem-and-solution

Problem solving essays regularly come as part of the writing assignments that focus on hot issues, policies and events. Usually these essays have two parts: a full explanation of the nature of the problem and justification of the problem's importance, followed by an analysis of solutions and their likelihood of success.

Useful expressions:

The real conditional is a useful way to talk about both problems and solutions. Also you can use some phrases to link problems with solutions.

> *Many arguments can be avoided if you think before you speak.*
> *In order to resolve the problems, …*
> *To meet this need, …*
> *One solution / approach / answer is …*
> *One thing we can do is …*

Sample 5-5-1

Drug Abuse

Drug abuse is rife in many countries. Billions of dollars are spent internationally preventing drug use, treating addicts and fighting drug-related crime. Although drugs threaten many societies, their effects can also be combated successfully. This essay looks at some of the effects of drug use on society and suggests some solutions to the problem.

Drug abuse causes multiple problems for countries and communities. The medical and psychological effects are very obvious. Addicts cannot function as normal members of society. They neglect or abuse their families and eventually require expensive treatment or hospitalization.

The second effect is on crime. Huge police resources are needed to fight smuggling and dealing. Criminal gangs and mafia underworlds develop with the money from drugs.

However, the menace of drugs can be fought. Education is the first battle. Children need to be told at home and in school about drugs. People need to be aware of the effects so that they can avoid this problem.

A second approach is to increase police manpower and create effective laws to stop dealers. However, the main target should be the user: Families and counselors need to talk to children and people at risk. Parents need to look at their children and help them to become responsible. Worthwhile jobs and housing are also needed to give people a role in society.

In conclusion, although the problem of drugs may seem impossible to eliminate, there are concrete steps that can be taken to weaken the hold of drugs on society. The danger from drugs is too great to ignore for us and our children.

Sample 5-5-2

Overpopulation in Large Cities

Many countries of the world are currently experiencing problems caused by rapidly growing populations in urban areas, and both governments and individuals have a duty to find ways to overcome these problems.

Overpopulation can lead to overcrowding and poor quality housing in many large cities. Poorly heated or damp housing could cause significant health problems, resulting in illness, such as bronchitis or pneumonia. Another serious consequence of overcrowding is a rising crime rate as poor living conditions may lead young people in particular to take desperate measures and turn to crime or drugs.

In terms of solutions, I believe the government should be largely responsible. Firstly, it is vital that the state provide essential housing and healthcare for all its citizens. Secondly, setting up community projects to help foster more community spirit and help keep young people off the street is a good idea. For example, youth clubs or evening classes for teenagers would keep them occupied. Finally, more effective policing of inner city areas would also be beneficial.

Naturally, individuals should also act responsibly to address these problems and the motivation to do this would hopefully arise if the measures described above are put into place by the government. This is because it will encourage people to have more pride in their own community and improve the situation.

Therefore, it is clear that the problems caused by overpopulation in urban areas are very serious. Yet if governments and individuals share a collective responsibility, then it may well become possible to offer some solutions.

Sample 5-5-3

Early School Leavers

In the UAE, many students fail to complete their basic schooling. This can cause serious problems for the individual, their families and the country. In this essay, I will examine the reasons why students leave school early and suggest some possible solutions

There are many reasons why students leave school early. Family problems are one cause. If parents are divorced, no one may be taking responsibility for the child. If parents are uneducated, there may be little encouragement to do homework or to stay in school. Financial factors are also important. Some students want to work in order to support their families. In contrast, others may have family businesses and not see any benefit in obtaining a high school certificates. Perhaps the main reason why students drop out is for academic reasons. For many students, school is stifling and boring. The curriculum does not challenge them or grab their attention and they are unable to be creative. Others have learning difficulties that need specialist help.

The problem of school drop-out can be reduced by using several strategies. First, educational authorities have to work closely with parents to monitor attendance. They need to follow up and determine the reasons for a student's absence. In some countries, parents are fined if the children are not attending. Schools also need social workers who can respond to family problems. A second approach is to implement changes in the curriculum so that school is more interesting for students at risk of dropping out. This could mean new methods of teaching or new subjects and facilities in the school. Thirdly, some financial help could be made available in a country like the UAE to encourage students with financial problems to stay in school.

As can be seen, there is no one solution to the problem of school drop-outs. Educational authorities, parents and schools need to work closely together to find the reason for each student's decision to leave school, and to try to do as much as possible to encourage them to stay in the system.

5.6　Expository Essay of Comparison and Contrast

Comparison and contrast is a method used to explain what is similar and what is different about two or more things. The purpose of comparison is to show how two things are alike and the opposite is true of contrast: the paragraph is to show how two things are different. In academic writing, comparison and contrast paragraphs are more often used to support the evaluation of two persons, places, things or ideas. There are usually two ways to organize comparison-contrast paragraphs. One is **block organization**, subject by subject, which discusses all the points of the first subject and then compare or contrast those same points to the other. The second method is **point by point organization**, which discusses one point of both subjects, then another point of both subjects.

Useful expressions:

similarly; likewise; also; too; as; equal(ly); the same; just like; both...and; neither...nor; in contrast; however; but; yet; while; whereas; although; even though; unlike; differ; different from; on the other hand

Sample 5-6-1

Right Brain and Left Brain

The left and right sides of your brain process information in different ways. The left side is logical, rational, linear and verbal. The right side, on the other hand, processes information intuitively, emotionally, creatively and visually. Left brains think in words, whereas right brains think in pictures. People who depend more on the left side of their brain are list makers and analysts. They are detailed, careful and organized. In contrast, right-brained people are visual, intuitive and sensual. When a left-brained person has to make an important decision, he or she makes a mental list of all the factors involved and arrives at a decision only after careful analysis. When a right-brained person has to make the same decision, on the other hand, he or she is more likely to base it on intuition and feelings. For example, a left-brained automobile shopper will consider a car's cost, fuel efficiency and resale value, whereas a right-brained shopper bases a decision on how shiny the chrome is, how soft the seats are and how smoothly the car drives. Of course, no one is 100 percent left-brained or 100 percent right-brained. Although one side may be stronger, both sides normally work together.

Sample 5-6-2

Frogs and Toads

Most of the people find it difficult to differentiate a frog from a toad. They normally mix them up. Although they seem so similar in appearance, they certainly have numerous dissimilarities too.

Frogs are found in many different shapes, sizes, colors and textures. Frogs have smooth, wet skin. They live most of the time in or near water. They have different eye colors including brown, silver, green, gold and red along with different shapes and sizes of pupil. Some of the frogs have sticky padding on their feet while others have webbed feet. It is obvious that not even all the frogs have the same qualities.

Toads too have numerous shapes, sizes and texture, but they don't have much variety in color. Toads are chubby and have warty skin. They do spend some of their time in water, but they live in moist places like woods, fields and gardens. Their pupils do have different shapes, sizes and colors, but generally they are egg-shaped, small and black. Usually they have webbed feet.

Toads and frogs have the same way to catch and eat food. Both of them use their tongue to gulp down the prey. But a frog has a crest of very small cone teeth around the upper jaw edge to seize the food, but a toad doesn't have any teeth at all. They eat almost the same foods as frogs like bugs, insects, fish, etc.

To sum up, frogs and toads do seem similar, but they have several different qualities regarding shape, size, color and texture. So it is crystally clear that people mistake while figuring out the difference between a frog and toad. It is needed that one should learn how a frog differs from a toad.

Sample 5-6-3

Innovative Education

The term "innovative education" has been presented to scientific community by American pedagogue James Botkin about twenty years ago and received numerous and rather controversial responses, for it suggested complete and irreversible revision of the principles traditional educational theories consider to be axiomatic.

To begin with, while traditional education considers the main value of educational process to be the knowledge transferred to the student, Botkin's innovative education presents the knowledge as a means rather than an end, at the same time orienting at the development of the student's personality through knowledge. It is less concerned with controlling the educational process, trying to create circumstances in which the student would establish his or her own goals and achieve them, while transforming his or her own self and self-regulating the studying process.

Traditional education represents in itself more or less stable structure, without undergoing dramatic differences in the course of years. The accumulation of knowledge goes on, of course, but only in the subjects where it is impossible to avoid, for example, history and literature, which are being expanded all the time. Curriculum for exact sciences, like physics or mathematics, may not change for decades. Botkin offers another decision, which presupposes that educational system is a dynamic and ever-changing structure that is being regrouped and renewed constantly, with new programs and educational disciplines appearing all the time.

As opposed to the reproductive nature of traditional education (the student perceives information and reproduces it), innovative education is supposed to be only and specifically creative process. It should teach students to create text irrespectively of its subject, understand information even if it has never been perceived by the student yet, and solve any problems by means of independent thinking rather than applying pre-existing, memorized solutions.

It also cancels the long-lasting tradition of "teacher-student" relationship as "superior-inferior," making both the teacher and the student equal participants of educational process, who work on one and the same task in cooperation, rather than submission. Any kind of outside control is supposed to be harmful for the process and, therefore, abolished, with its place taken by self-control, mutual control and coordination.

Of course, the self-sufficient system of education based on equality of teacher and student may look really alluring, but all the same, it is more of a utopia than reality. Botkin idealizes children and thinks that it is possible to create such a system; reality would most likely say "no."

5.7 Expository Essay of Exemplification

Exemplification is a common and efficient pattern of development in expository writing. As William Ruehlmann says, "The best way to reveal a problem, phenomenon or social circumstance is to illustrate it with a single, specific instance" (*Stalking the Feature Story*, 1978). It involves presenting the reader with numerous examples to clarify, define, explain or prove something. Not only do these examples illustrate and explain the topic sentence, but they also make your writing more interesting and more convincing.

To write a good exemplification essay, the writer should first develop a general statement—the thesis. The key is that the thesis should always have a generalization that needs to be defended. Then, carefully select examples to support a generalization about a thesis. That is, the examples must be the most appealing, vivid and appropriate ones. They could be specific ones about your personal experience or typical ones common to everyone. Sometimes you can even use hypothetical examples in imaginary situations if the other examples are not strong enough to prove the point. But always remember the examples must be relevant.

Useful expressions:

for example; for instance; such as; like; namely; that is; a case in point is...; take ...as an example; to illustrate

Sample 5-7-1

The Other Side of Television

Television has exposed a world of violence, drugs and sexual immorality to our youths, causing them to be apathetic towards these issues. Many television shows have made at least one of the three aspects: violence, drugs and sexual immorality, a normalcy.

"The Simpsons" is a show that is enjoyed by many teens. This show depicts violence as something comedic. Regularly, in this show, the father chokes his son at least once, and the children watch a cartoon show called "Itchy and Scratchy," in which a cat and mouse try to kill each other. Our youths today find this violence funny. When they encounter violence in real life, they do not consider it serious because they experience it every day on the television.

Characters in television shows such as "Married with Children" smoke, and although there are commercials advertising against smoking more than ever, smoking on the television gives our youths a different message. This advertises for the cigarette companies for practically free.

In "The Drew Carey Show," all the main characters spend their free time in a bar drinking. They even make and sell their very own beer. "Cheers" is another show that advocates drinking. Most of the show takes place in a bar. These characters in television shows have influence on our youths.

Sexual immorality has also become common, which is exemplified by a show called "Friends." "Friends" depicts each of their characters as people who sleep around. Sex is an integrated part of their lives and is expected when any one of the characters has a significant other. "Undeclared" revolves around college life in which college students have sex with each other "just for fun." Adolescents of today model their behavior after characters like these who live in worlds of violence, drugs and sexual immorality, and they do not realize that what they are doing is wrong because to our youths, whatever they see and hear on television is right.

Sample 5-7-2

Conscience of the Universities Presidents

Universities presidents once spoke their conscience on matters of great public importance. In the early 1950s, many protested the loyalty oaths that required faculty members to forswear membership in the Communist Party.

One of the most courageous critics of McCarthyism was Nathan Pusey, first as president of Lawrence College in Senator Joseph McCarthy's hometown of Appleton, Wisconsin, then as president of Harvard. In the 1960s, some university presidents openly opposed the war in Vietnam. Even at the cost of donor support, Yale president Kingman Brewster Jr. publicly contested the war and decried the inequities in the draft. He permitted protest demonstrations and skillfully kept the Yale campus open and relatively calm.

5.8 Expository Essay of Listing

Listing is presenting a series of details or facts. It "may compile a history, gather evidence, order and organize phenomena, present an agenda of apparent formlessness and express a multiplicity of voices and experiences…" "Each unit in a list possesses an individual significance but also a specific meaning by virtue of its membership with the other units in the compilation (though this is not to say that the units are always equally significant)." (Robert E. Belknap, *The List: The Uses and Pleasures of Cataloguing*. Yale Univ. Press, 2004). That is to say, the items in a list are usually arranged in parallel form or in an order of importance. Listing can be used with other developing patterns such as cause-effect, problem-solution, classification and so on.

Useful expressions:

first; second; third; finally; another; still another; in addition; besides; moreover; for one thing; for another; alternatively

Sample 5-8-1

How to Keep Healthy

More and more research is showing that the key to lifelong good health is what experts call "lifestyle medicine"—making simple changes in diet, exercise and stress management. To help you turn that knowledge into results, we've put together this manageable list of health and wellness action steps.

1. Think positive and focus on gratitude

Research shows a healthy positive attitude helps build a healthier immune system and boosts overall health. Your body believes what you think, so focus on the positive.

2. Eat your vegetables

Shoot for five servings of vegetables a day—raw, steamed or stir-fried. A diet high in vegetables is associated with a reduced risk of developing cancers of the lung, colon, breast, cervix, esophagus, stomach, bladder, pancreas and ovary. And many of the most powerful phytonutrients are the ones with the boldest colors—such as broccoli, cabbage, carrots, tomatoes, grapes and leafy greens.

3. Set a "5-meal ideal"

What, when and how much you eat can keep both your metabolism and your energy levels steadily elevated, so you'll have more all-day energy. A "5 meal ideal" will help you manage your weight, keep your cool, maintain your focus and avoid cravings.

4. Exercise daily

Did you know that daily exercise can reduce all of the biomarkers of aging? This includes improving eyesight, normalizing blood pressure, improving lean muscle, lowering cholesterol and improving bone density. If you want to live well and live longer, you must exercise! Studies show that even 10 minutes of exercise makes a difference—so do something! Crank the stereo and dance in your living room. Sign up for swing dancing or ballroom-dancing lessons. Walk to the park with your kids or a neighbor you'd like to catch up with. Jump rope or play hopscotch. Spin a hula hoop. Play water volleyball. Bike to work. Jump on a trampoline. Go for a hike.

5. Get a good night's sleep

If you have trouble sleeping, try relaxation techniques such as meditation and yoga. Or eat a small bedtime snack of foods shown to help shift the body and mind into sleep mode: whole grain cereal with milk, oatmeal, cherries or chamomile tea. Darken your room more and turn your clock away from you. Write down worries or stressful thoughts to get them out of your head and onto the page. This will help you put them into perspective so you can quit worrying about them.

Sample 5-8-2

Life on the Mars

In a sense, scientists' ideas about early Mars are more uncertain than they have ever been. This doubt comes to the fore when researchers address the question of liquid water. The presence or absence of liquid water is fundamental to geologic processes, climate change and the origin of life. The early valley networks and the later flood channels attest to an abundance of water. The evidence for early rainfall suggests that the atmosphere was once much denser. But spacecraft have found no evidence for deposits of carbonate minerals, which would be the vestige expected from an early dense carbon dioxide atmosphere.

At this point, scientists have three main hypotheses. Perhaps the early atmosphere was indeed thick. The planet might have had lakes, even oceans, free of ice. Robert A. Craddock of the National Air and Space Museum and Alan D. Howard of the University of Virginia recently suggested that the carbon dioxide was lost to space or locked up in carbonate minerals that have so far escaped detection. Intriguingly, Mars Odyssey spectra have revealed small amounts of carbonate in the dust.

Alternatively, perhaps Mars had a fairly thin atmosphere. It was a wintry world. Any standing bodies of water were covered in ice. Snow might have fallen, recharging the groundwater and leading to temporary trickles of water across the surface. Steven M. Clifford of the Lunar and Planetary Science Institute in Houston, among others, has conjectured that melting under a glacier or a thick layer of permafrost could also have recharged subterranean water sources. Although Mars was bitterly cold, periodic bursts of relatively warmer temperatures could have reinvigorated the planet. Orbital shifts, similar to those that trigger ice ages on Earth, drove these climate cycles. Head, John F. Mustard of Brown and others have pointed to the latitude dependence of the ice and dust cover as evidence for climate change.

Finally, perhaps the climate cycles were insufficient to make Mars warm enough to sustain liquid waters. The planet had warm conditions for only brief periods after major impacts. Each such impact deposited water-rich material and pumped enough heat and water into the atmosphere to permit rain. Soon, though, the planet returned to its usual frozen state. Victor Baker of the University of Arizona has argued that the intensive volcanism in the Tharsis region periodically made early Mars quite a temperate place.

It is also very possible that none of these options is correct. We simply do not yet know enough about early Mars to have any real understanding of its climate. We must wait for future exploration.

Ex. 5-1 *Read the following paragraphs and see how different methods of development are used*

The Olympic symbol consists of five interlocking rings. The rings represent the five continents — Africa, Asia, Europe, North America and South America — from which athletes come to compete in the games. The rings are colored black, blue, green, red and yellow. At least one of these colors is found in the flag of every country sending athletes to compete in the Olympic games.	Description

The Olympic games began as athletic festivals to honor the Greek gods. The most important festival was held in the valley of Olympia to honor Zeus, the king of the gods. It was this festival that became the Olympic games in 776 B.C. These games were ended in A.D. 394 by the Roman Emperor who ruled Greece. No Olympic games were held for more than 1,500 years. Then the modern Olympics began in 1896. Almost 300 male athletes competed in the first modern Olympics. In the games held in 1900, female athletes were allowed to compete. The games have continued every four years since 1896 except during World War II, and they will most likely continue for many years to come.	Sequence
The modern Olympics is very unlike the ancient Olympic games. Individual events are different. While there were no swimming races in the ancient games, for example, there were chariot races. There were no female contestants and all athletes competed in the nude. Of course, the ancient and modern Olympics are also alike in many ways. Some events, such as the javelin and discus throws, are the same. Some people say that cheating, professionalism and nationalism in the modern games are a disgrace to the Olympic tradition. But according to the ancient Greek writers, there were many cases of cheating, nationalism and professionalism in their Olympics too.	Comparison
There are several reasons why so many people attend the Olympic games or watch them on television. One reason is tradition. The name Olympics and the torch and flame remind people of the ancient games. People can escape the ordinariness of daily life by attending or watching the Olympics. They like to identify with someone else's individual sacrifice and accomplishment. National pride is another reason, and an athlete's or a team's hard earned victory becomes a nation's victory. There are national medal counts and people keep track of how many medals their country's athletes have won.	Cause and Effect
One problem with the modern Olympics is that it has become very big and expensive to operate. The city or country that hosts the games often loses a lot of money. A stadium, pools and playing fields must be built for the athletic events and housing is needed for the athletes who come from around the world. And all of these facilities are used for only 2 weeks! In 1984, Los Angeles solved these problems by charging a fee for companies who wanted to be official sponsors of the games. Companies like McDonald's paid a lot of money to be part of the Olympics. Many buildings that were already built in the Los Angeles area were also used. The Coliseum where the 1932 games were held was used again and many colleges and universities in the area became playing and living sites.	Problem and Solution

Ex. 5-2 *Read the following passage and answer the questions.*

1. What important information seems to be missing from the introductory paragraph?

2. Which sentence from the body paragraph might be placed more effectively in the introduction?

3. Identify the transitional words or phrases which are used to guide the reader clearly from step to step in the body paragraph.

4. Suggest how the single long body paragraph might be effectively divided into two or three shorter paragraphs.

5. Do you think the warnings in the concluding paragraph have been placed in the right place? If not, where do you think they should have been placed, and why?

How to Make a Sand Castle

For young and old alike, a trip to the beach means relaxation, adventure, and a temporary escape from the worries and responsibilities of ordinary life. Whether swimming or surfing, tossing a volleyball or just snoozing in the sand, a visit to the beach means fun. The only equipment you need is a twelve-inch deep pail, a small plastic shovel, and plenty of moist sand.

Making a sandcastle is a favorite project of beach-goers of all ages. Begin by digging up a large amount of sand (enough to fill at least six pails) and arranging it in a pile. Then, scoop the sand into your pail, patting it down and leveling it off at the rim as you do. You can now construct the towers of your castle by placing one pailful of sand after another face down on the area of the beach that you have staked out for yourself. Make four towers, placing each mound twelve inches apart in a square. This done, you are ready to build the walls that connect the towers. Scoop up the sand along the perimeter of the fortress and arrange a wall six inches high and twelve inches long between each pair of towers in the square. By scooping up the sand in this fashion, you will not only create the walls of the castle, but you will also be digging out the moat that surrounds it. Now, with a steady hand, cut a one-inch square block out of every other inch along the circumference of each tower. Your spatula will come in handy here. Of course, before doing this, you should use the spatula to smooth off the tops and sides of the walls and towers.

You have now completed your very own sixteenth-century sandcastle. Though it may not last for centuries or even until the end of the afternoon, you can still take pride in your handicraft. Do make sure, however, that you have chosen a fairly isolated spot in which to work; otherwise, your masterpiece may be trampled by beach bums and children. Also, make a note on the high tides so that you have enough time to build your fortress before the ocean arrives to wash it all away.

Ex 5-3. Rearrange the following sentences from a process passage. Make your paragraph flow smoothly by adding time order signal words or phrases at the beginning of some of the sentences.

1. Find the computers that contain the library's catalogs.
2. Locate the books on the library shelves by their call numbers.
3. Be prepared to show your library card at the checkout desk.
4. In the age of computers, finding a book in the library has become very easy.
5. In the book catalog, type the topic you are seeking information about in the space labeled "Subject."
6. There are two catalogs: one for books and one for periodicals (magazines, newspapers, and so on).
7. Write down the title and call number of each book that you want.
8. Scroll through the entries for the books that are displayed on the computer screen, and determine which ones seem the most relevant.
9. Take the books to the checkout desk.

Ex. 5-4. Work with your partner or a small group. You are a travel agent and need to help a client make a decision on a vacation destination between Alaska and Hawaii for her summer. You've gathered some information about the two places. Organize the information by filling in the chart and prepare a report.

The information you have gathered:
1. The quality of hotels in Alaska is quite good.
2. It often rains during the summer in Hawaii.
3. The temperature is perfect in Alaska during the summer.
4. Hawaii has Volcano National Park and Wairnea Canyon.
5. Accommodations in Alaska vary from basic to luxury.
6. The beaches in Hawaii are among the most beautiful in the world.
7. The glaciers in Alaska are awesome.
8. There is a wide range of excellent hotels and condos in Hawaii, from luxury to budget priced.
9. Alaska has the Chugach Mountains and Mount McKinley, the highest mountain in North America.
10. It seldom rains during the summer in Alaska.
11. It can be hot and humid in Hawaii in the summer.
12. There is no humidity in Alaska.

Main topics	Alaska	Hawaii
Accommodation		
Climate		
Natural beauty		

Ex.5-5 *Choose one or more of the following topics and write a comparison or contrast paragraph, using either block organization or point-by-point organization.*
1. Action movie/romantic movie.
2. Living in a dormitory/renting an apartment.
3. Golf/tennis.
4. Hybrid car/gasoline car.

Ex. 5-6 *Choose a word or holiday from your country and write a paragraph to define it and explain its meaning or significance.*

Ex. 5-7 *Talk with your partner and tell him/her how to do a thing that you know well. Brainstorm all the steps that need to be followed. Remember to use transitional words.*

Ex. 5-8 *Talk about your problems with your partner and then work together to brainstorm solutions* to your problems. Select the best one or ones which are practical and logical to write into a paragraph.

Ex. 5-9 Use your own criteria to classify friends and foods. Then compare your result with your partner's.

Ex. 5-10 Choose one or more of the topics to write about.
1. How is your generation different from your parents' generation?
2. What are the responsibilities of the mother and the father for raising children in China?
3. It has become increasingly difficult for college graduates to find jobs. What are the causes? Can you give some suggestions?
4. What factors contribute to job satisfaction? How to meet the expectation of job satisfaction for all workers?
5. The effects of growing up with a personal computer.
6. Why are more and more students taking online classes?
7. What is success in your eyes?

Chapter Six
Argumentation

Introduction

Argumentative or persuasive writing is an important form of human communications, in which the author expresses a point of view on a subject and supports it with evidence. The purpose of exposition is to inform; the purpose of augmentation, on the other hand, is to convince. That is, augmentation not only gives information but also presents an argument with the pros (supporting ideas) and cons (opposing ideas) of an argumentative issue. In an augmentative essay, the author should clearly take his/her stand and write as if he/she is trying to persuade an opposing audience to adopt new beliefs or behavior. So the primary objective of augmentation is to convince or persuade the reader. Speeches on policies, editorials of newspapers, articles on political or theoretical questions, and various proposals are often argumentative.

Some conventions of argumentative essays

(1) Since argumentative writing is to persuade, it should contain an argument, often called a "claim" or "thesis statement," backed up with evidence that supports the idea. In other words, it should have a debatable point. Look at the following theses:

 * *We should decide whether we want a bicycle or a car.* —It is not a good one since the author's stand is not clear.

 √ *If we are under the age of 30 and want a healthy life, we should definitely get a bicycle instead of a car.*

 * *Are you one of those who think cheating is not good for students?* —A question cannot be an argument.

 √ *Cheating poses a threat to students' learning.*

 * *Considering its geological position, Turkey has an important geopolitical role in the EU.* —

Facts cannot be arguments.

    √ *Considering its geopolitical role, we can clearly say that the EU cannot be without Turkey.*

    * *I feel that writing an argumentative essay is definitely a challenging task.* —Feelings or personal preference cannot be supported; we cannot persuade other people.

    √ *Writing augmentative essays is a must for freshmen.*

(2) Do not stop with only a point. You have to back up your point with evidence. The strength of the evidence, and use of it, can make or break the argument. Valid evidence includes common knowledge, specific examples, facts, statistics and quotations from authorities. Look at the following evidence using examples:

    School failures can also become great men later in their lives. Famous inventor Thomas Edison, for instance, did so poorly in his first years of school that his teacher warned his parents that he'd never be a success at anything. Similarly, Henry Ford, the father of the auto industry, had trouble in school with both reading and writing. But perhaps the best example is Albert Einstein, whose parents and teachers suspected that he was retarded because he responded to questions so slowly and in a stuttering voice. Einstein's high school record was poor in everything but math, and he failed his college entrance exams the first time. Even out of school the man had trouble holding a job—until he announced the theory of relativity.

(3) One way to strengthen the argument and show that the author has a deep understanding of the issue being discussed is to anticipate and address counterarguments or objections. By considering what someone who disagrees might have to say about the argument, the author shows that things have been thought through, thus preparing the audience for accepting his/her argument. Before we start saying that the opponents are wrong, we should specify their opposing ideas. Otherwise, it would be like hitting the other person with eyes closed. We should see clearly what we are hitting and be prepared beforehand so that he cannot hit us back. We can do this by knowing what we are refuting. Look at the following refutation:

    Some people may say that adolescents should not leave university education because they are not physically and psychologically mature enough to cope with the problems of the real world. However, they forget one fact: adolescents can vote or start driving at the age of 18 (in some countries even before that age!), which proves that they are considered physically and psychologically mature at that age.

(4) Argumentative writing requires careful organization. Since all argumentative topics have pros and cons, before starting writing, it is better to make a list of these ideas and choose the most suitable ones among them for supporting and refuting. There are four possible organization patterns:

Pattern 1	Pattern 2
Thesis statement	Thesis statement
Pro idea 1	Con(s) + Refutation(s)

	continued
Pattern 1	**Pattern 2**
Pro idea 2	Pro idea 1
Pro idea 3	Pro idea 2
Conclusion	Conclusion
Pattern 3	**Pattern 4**
Thesis statement	Thesis statement
Pro idea 1	Con idea 1 → Refutation
Pro idea 2	Con idea 2 → Refutation
Con(s) + Refutation(s)	Con idea 3 → Refutation
Conclusion	Conclusion

6.1 Argumentative Essay—Pattern 1

Sample 6-1-1

Private Cars Should Not Be Encouraged

The number of private cars is on the rise in our country. Some people think that private cars should be encouraged. Others argue that private cars should be limited. I think that too many private cars may create endless problems though they can bring much convenience and comfort.

First, cars often produce air pollution and fill the cities with unbearable noises. Second, most of the important cities in the world suffer from traffic congestion. In fact, any advantage gained in comfort is often cancelled out by the frustration caused by traffic jams within the city, endless queues of cars crawling bumper to bumper through all the main streets. Third, to own a private car in China will not only cost you a fortune, but also bring you all kinds of trouble: getting a license plate, keeping the machine in good maintenance, finding a parking place at night, etc. What is worse, cars are the main cause of traffic accidents. All over the world thousands upon thousands of people are killed or injured every year. Traffic accidents caused by cars not only bring deaths and injury, but also make people suffer mentally and physically. In addition, our country has a very large population. If everyone had a car, all the roads would be crowded with cars!

Therefore, I think the number of private cars should be limited. We should try to find a safer means of transport that will bring joy and comfort rather than injury and death. (247 words)

Sample 6-1-2

The British Police Should Carry Guns

Unlike the police in most other countries, the British police are noted for not being routinely armed, and their armament is limited to the baton. But as gun crime is on the rise, the police should be authorised to carry weapons to protect themselves as well as the public.

The safety of police officers would be the first priority. The police would occasionally come up against armed criminals. Some criminals will act violently against the police in order to avoid legal punishment. If they do not have the appropriate weapon to defend themselves against guns, their lives may be in danger. Therefore, the police should be armed so that they can protect themselves and the public.

Also, police officers should carry weapons in order to promptly attend to an incident or offence. When a violent crime is committed, police must first arm themselves before attending the scene of the crime. Since it threatens further loss of life, it is imperative that police should get to the scene as soon as possible. But it's no good having a police officer patrolling on foot a block away from a violent crime if they aren't armed, and therefore have to go and get their firearm before attending the scene.

Furthermore, the police should be a threatening symbol to all criminals. Their main purpose is to enforce the law, so if police were to use the arms to protect their lives, or the lives of law-abiding citizens, then the potential criminals will be effectively deterred from committing crimes.

In conclusion, it is the duty of the police officer to protect the well-being of the general public, therefore they should be granted the right to carry guns so they can perform that duty with maximum effect. (291 words)

6.2　Argumentative Essay—Pattern 2

Sample 6-2-1

Homeschooling

Most children go to school for education because it is generally believed that in a regular school, kids get mingled with their peers and teachers and in the process acquire social skills that are important when they progress into adult life. Meanwhile, still some parents prefer to educate their children at home, especially with the easy access to information and knowledge due to the availability of computer and Internet.

Some critics have criticized that homeschooling does not fulfill the social aspect of education. Since the child is studying alone at home, it does not give him/her the opportunity to pick up social skills. However, studies have shown quite the opposite. Public school children are put under fiercely competitive school environments. The net result is that they lack the confidence to initiate or hold a conversation. They do not know how to interact with other age group people.

On the other hand, homeschooling children are more aware of the implications and purpose of their learning. They are also able to make intelligent comments and are more attentive when studying.

Some studies also concluded that public school goers pick up bad influences from their peers, while homeschooling children are shielded from such negative influences.

In my own opinion, homeschooling children are better prepared with the tools necessary to face *the world. Being shielded from negative influences from their peers plus the positive influences from parents will help them to become more versatile and well-rounded individuals. (244 words)*

Sample 6-2-2

Should Children Be Forced to Obey Rules?

Most parents want to help their children learn to behave well and achieve success in the future, so they set many rules for young children and expect absolute obedience from their children. However, I do not believe this practice is justified.

It can be argued that rules are the prerequisite for discipline and order. Children usually lack self-control and they are inclined to develop acceptable social behaviors if they have specific rules to follow. Proponents hold that if children are not required to follow regulations, how can you expect them to abide by law when they grow up? However, we mustn't ignore the fact that such discipline is maintained at the price of more valuable qualities we expect from our children.

Obeying rules is detrimental to children's independence and initiative. Since they are used to following directions, they will be totally at a loss once the instructions are gone. They may not have the courage to face a difficult situation and solve the problem by themselves. This will lead to frustrations in adult life and failures in their future career.

Also, they may lack imagination and creativity. Believing authority, they always follow routines and do not try to approach a problem in more ways than one. Critical thinking is not cultivated and many inventions are made impossible.

Furthermore, although some shortcuts are offered in directions, children lose the precious chances to learn from their own mistakes and failures. While exploring the truth, children can accumulate much knowledge and become mature in forming their judgment and world-views.

Last but not least, punishment will usually follow failures to observe certain rules, which may bring psychological damage to children. In the long run, they may lose confidence and become timid. When opportunities come, they may easily give up and they may never reach their full potential.

For the above reasons, children should be encouraged to make their own decisions and thus they will become more adaptable and competitive in their future work and life. (331 words)

Sample 6-2-3

Should Students Be Encouraged to Evaluate Their Teachers?

Traditionally, teachers symbolize authority. Obedient and respectful, students are accustomed to taking the teachers as they are, accepting what they are taught and doing whatever they are told to do. With the implementation of educational reform at all levels, evaluating teachers has been proposed as a means of improving the quality of education. I believe both teachers and students will benefit from this practice.

Opponents argue that such practices might give rise to indiscipline and disrespect for teachers.

By adopting this critical method, students might be encouraged to become eager to challenge and criticize. They might even take advantage of this well-meant attempt to achieve their own purposes such as having less homework. In that case, formal education will no longer be a serious matter. However, as the major participants and beneficiaries of education, students should be entitled to voice their opinions about how they are taught.

First of all, encouraging learners to assess their instructors' performance may help the latter gain a better understanding of how the teaching is received and perceived. The student-centered teaching model enables teachers to find out whether or not they should adjust their speed, speak louder, present more detailed explanations, or even switch to a more suitable teaching approach. More importantly, this practice would cultivate students' independent and critical thinking, invite more active involvement from them, and help them gain a deeper understanding of their lessons. In the long run, students will become autonomous learners, which is the ultimate goal of education. Finally, feedback from the students may also make it possible for the school to reward the qualified teachers and dismiss the incompetent and irresponsible ones, thus establishing a good reputation as a school.

Based on the above discussion and analysis, this practice is feasible and we should trust the students, especially college students, who are mature enough to take it seriously and offer fair judgment. Hopefully, the assessment will contribute to better communication between the teachers and students and eventually the improvement of education. (333 words)

6.3 Argumentative Essay—Pattern 3

Sample 6-3-1

We Should Use Formal Examination as a Means of Assessment

Examination has long played an important role in education. Although a growing number of people have begun to challenge its reliability, I think examination has more advantages. There are numerous reasons why I hold this opinion, and I would explore a few of the most important ones here.

Certainly no other reason in my decision is more crucial than the following one. Examination is important because it is an effective means of assessment. How can teachers and parents know how well the students are learning? How can students themselves know? There is only one answer: examination. Some schools have tried using other forms of assessment alone, but the individual attention required makes it too time-consuming. Besides, the individualized evaluation is not dependable and it also makes regional and national assessment of students impossible.

There is another factor that deserves some words here. Examination is necessary because it requires students to learn facts, which are important for the students. Unfortunately, learning facts is now often regarded as out-of-date. It is said that students should think for themselves. But storing facts is a prerequisite for independent and critical thinking. No one can think with an empty mind.

Finally, examination is vital because they make students work hard. Laziness is part of human nature. It is not helpful for students to learn. Examination can make students work hard and help them learn to make full use of their study time.

On the other hand, we must say that examination also has some disadvantages. First, it can't assess the whole qualities of the students. Secondly, it can generate an unhealthy spirit of jealousy and competition. We can't use examination as the sole evaluation of students. But without examination, it will be harder for educational institutions to select qualified candidates.

No matter what other means of assessment we add, examination must remain a vital part of schooling. (312 words)

Sample 6-3-2

Will TV Affect Children's Creativity?

As science and technology advances, television, as a powerful invention in the 20th century, is becoming unbelievably popular in people's life. People can keep track of the current affairs and appreciate the diverse programs right at home. As to my opinion of it, television will not weaken children's creativity.

To begin with, television is the most effective means to inform children of the latest news and scientific improvement all over the world. Television reveals the recent development of some researches, such as the new computing technology, clone technology and genetic breakthroughs, which can inspire the imagination of children and motivate them to conduct relevant experiments, making new findings and breakthroughs in their study.

Moreover, some programs like adventures and geography can enlarge children's knowledge. With the emergence of information technology, the knowledge presented in textbooks cannot cater for children's curiosity any more. Children need to learn wider knowledge and know more about our world. Programs like adventures can cultivate children's creativity and the ability to tackle difficulty; programs like geography can teach children knowledge about different countries in the world and initiate their aspiration to know about the nature; programs about science can inspire children's interest in science and technology.

Admittedly, the inappropriate programs on television somehow play a negative role in the shaping of children. The films containing violence, crimes and pornography contents tempt children to go astray. However, proper education and parental guidance may well minimize and even eliminate the negative influence.

In a word, it is my strong belief that television will not impair children's creativity as is asserted. Nevertheless, the government and the whole society should make joint efforts to eliminate the unhealthy contents on TV and ensure that the children grow in a favorable environment. (292 words)

6.4　Argumentative Essay—Pattern 4

Sample 6-4-1

Animal Testing

Every day, thousands of people are saved from painful diseases and death by powerful medical drugs and treatments. This incredible gift of medicine would not be possible without animal testing. Despite these overwhelming benefits, however, some people are calling for animal testing to be banned because of alleged cruelty. This essay will outline the necessity of animal testing.

Those against the use of animal testing claim that it is inhumane to use animals in experiments. I disagree completely. It would be much more inhumane to test new drugs on children or adults. Even if it were possible, it would also take much longer to see potential effects because of the length of time we live compared to laboratory animals such as rats or rabbits.

Opponents of animal testing also claim that the results are not applicable to humans. This may be partly true. Some drugs have had to be withdrawn, despite testing. However, we simply do not have alternative methods of testing. Computer models are not advanced enough, and testing on plants is much less applicable to humans than tests on animals such as monkeys. Until we have a better system, we must use animal testing.

A further point often raised against animal testing is that it is cruel. Some of the tests certainly seem painful, but the great majority of people on this planet eat meat or wear leather without any guilt. Where is their sympathy for animals? Furthermore, animals clearly do not feel the same way as humans, and scientists are careful to minimize stress in the animals, even if this would damage their research.

I agree that we need to make sure that animals who are used for testing new products have the minimum of suffering. However, I am convinced that animal testing is necessary, and that it will continue to benefit humans in new and wonderful ways. (310 words)

6.5　More Samples of Argumentative Essays

Sample 6-5-1

Topic: Individuals do not need to improve the environment. Only government and big companies can make a difference. To what extent do you agree or disagree?

Environmental issues have been a big concern in the past decades. Every one knows if the environment is damaged, no one on Earth will escape the effects. It is true that the authorities and big companies have an essential role to play in combating environmental problems. However, it does not mean that individuals can do nothing in this great endeavor.

No doubt, some environmental problems are simply beyond individual effort, such as global *warming, industrial pollution, soil erosion, deforestation, sand and dust storms, etc., which call for commitment and cooperation from the government and big companies. For example, the government can impose strict controls over exhaust emission levels of motor vehicles, reduce pollution and improve energy efficiency through legislation and law enforcement. Also, to manufacturers, environmental concern should be given priority over economic growth in order to maintain sustainable development for human beings in the long run. For instance, they can adopt some recycling programs, safe disposal of toxic waste, and so on.*

However, the influence of individuals on environment cannot be ignored. If everyone contributes a little bit to the preservation of nature and environment, we can achieve amazing results. We can simply start with small things like saving electricity by using energy efficient lighting and using less air conditioning, conserving water by fixing leaking faucets and using water-efficient appliances, refusing plastic bags by bringing bags when shopping, riding bicycles or using public transportation to commute and taking the train instead of the airplane whenever possible.

Therefore, the government should take effective measures to handle environmental issues; the manufacturers and factories should consider social benefits as well as economic profits. Meanwhile, individuals should realize they have a crucial role to play in environmental protection and should always be environmentally conscious. If the government and people can join hands in solving environmental problems, our future generation can enjoy a healthy life and rich resources. (314 words)

Sample 6-5-2

Topic: *Some consider that history is of little or no use to us. Others believe that studying history helps us to understand the present. Discuss their views and give your own opinion.*

Things happened in the past, known as history, seem distant and irrelevant to some people. So they argue that today's world is new and complex and the past provides little guidance for living in the present. However, I firmly believe an understanding of the past helps us understand the situation of our contemporary world better.

Admittedly, we are now living in a society greatly different from our ancestors' and we are now facing many unprecedented problems such as political styles, international peace and security, global economy, environmental pollution, laid-off workers, stress from social competition. However, even though we cannot refer these complicated issues to history for direct solutions, history remains a great treasure for us human beings, through which we can gain valuable experience, which serves as a means of guiding the development of our society.

First of all, history is the collective memory of a specific group, such as a nation, a race or even a family. It can be regarded as important ties among generations. The heroes and events, in the history of a specific nation, make its descendants feel proud and promote the solidarity among people. Simply put, history is the root of our contemporary society.

Secondly, studying history can help us avoid repeating mistakes. Without guidance from the past, people have no idea which way is the best possible solution and which way will lead to the same failure as our ancestors. For instance, we can learn from the downfall of the Qing Dynasty that it can be a serious mistake to be isolated from the world and prohibit commerce and communication. This profound lesson teaches descendants that only an open mind and policy can promote the prosperity of a country.

Thirdly, we can accumulate valuable experience by examining how people coped with the similar problems in the past. Despite the complexity of modern problems and situations, the causes of problems may still remain the same and unchanged over extended periods of time. We can learn how these problems were worked out, which may cast light on effective and efficient solutions to current issues.

To sum up, the past to the contemporary society today, just like the map to a driver, can tell us which is a shorter route to the destination of success and well-being. (381 words)

Sample 6-5-3

Topic: International media such as TV, films and magazines have great impact on local cultures. Do you think their advantages outweigh the disadvantages?

Technology has now created the possibility of a global culture. The advances in communications and transportations have swept away the old national boundaries and shortened the physical distance among people. Meanwhile, international media and entertainment companies are shaping understandings, values and dreams of ordinary citizens wherever they live. In my view, although this cultural globalization has certain positive effects on nations, its negative impacts appear more prominent.

It is true that the international mass media have for the first time resulted in the majority of people sharing the same experiences. Films such as "Titanic" are known the world over and musicians and sports stars are celebrated all over the world. Many people believe this common ground brings people closer together, which may help foster friendship between nations and promote world peace.

However, local cultures and languages fall victim to a global culture. For example, few students in China like or even understand Beijing Opera; instead, they prefer Hollywood films and international stars. The cultural identity is gradually fading, which results in the loss of certain minority languages. Just as the world is becoming less biologically rich, it is also becoming less culturally and linguistically diverse.

Even worse, the global culture is actually a cultural monopoly. It is an indisputable fact that the United States dominates the traffic of information and ideas. American music, movies, television shows are so dominant that they are available almost everywhere on the earth and are influencing the tastes, lives and aspirations of every nation. In a way, this globalization is Americanization. As a result, some news broadcasts often represent the viewpoint of the owner rather than an objective opinion, so the public are unlikely to get a balanced perspective.

In the final analysis, in spite of the fact that a global culture offers some advantages, it is not wise to sacrifice the cultural diversity for this cultural uniformity. (312 words)

Sample 6-5-4
Topic: In some countries young people are encouraged to work or travel for a year between finishing high school and starting university studies. Discuss the advantages and disadvantages for young people to do this and your opinion.

It is quite common these days for young people in many countries to have a break from studying after graduating from high school. This trend is not restricted to rich students who have the money to travel, but is also evident among poorer students who choose to work and become economically independent for a period of time.

The reasons for this trend may involve the recognition that a young adult who passes directly from school to university is rather restricted in terms of general knowledge and experience of the world. By contrast, those who have spent some time earning a living or traveling to other places have a broader view of life and better personal resources to draw on. They tend to be more independent, which is a very important factor in academic study and research, as well as giving them an advantage in terms of coping with the challenges of student life.

However, there are certainly dangers in taking time off at that important age. Young adults may end up never returning to their studies or finding it difficult to readapt to an academic environment. They may think that it is better to continue in a particular job, or to do something completely different from a university course. But overall, I think this is less likely today, when academic qualifications are essential for getting a reasonable career.

My view is that young people should be encouraged to broaden their horizons. That is the best way for them to get a clear perspective of what they are hoping to do with their lives and why. Students with such a perspective are usually the most effective and motivated ones and taking a year off may be the best way to gain this. *(291 words)*

(Source: Cambridge IELTS 5: 165)

Ex. *Suggested topics for argumentative writing.*

a. Some people say that computers can translate all kinds of languages. Therefore, children do not need to learn foreign languages any more. What's your position?

b. Some people think the students should take the subjects which are decided by the authorities of the university. Others think that students can choose the subjects they prefer. Discuss the two situations and give your opinion.

c. Computer technology would replace the function of public library. Maintaining the public libraries is a waste of money because the computer technology is replacing its function. Do you agree or disagree?

d. More and more people use mobile phones or computers to communicate instead of letter-writing, so the skill of letter-writing will soon disappear completely. Do you agree or disagree?

e. Some people think that students benefit from going to private secondary schools. Others feel that private secondary schools have a negative effect on society as a whole. Discuss both sides. What is your opinion?

f. The advantages brought by the spread of English as a "global language" outweigh the disadvantages. To what extent do you agree or disagree?

g. Some children in rural places cannot have good school and medical facilities. To improve this situation, some people suggest that new teachers and doctors should be sent to rural places for a few years. Others, however, believe everyone has the free right to choose where to work. Discuss and give your own opinion.

h. It is not necessary for students to go to school, because more information is accessible on the Internet. Instead, children can study at home. Do you agree or disagree?

Chapter Seven

Illustration Description

Introduction

In presenting scientific research, the writer may need to put the research results in tables, graphs or charts, which enables the readers to have a better understanding of the scientific data. In some exams, the writing tasks also require the description and interpretation of statistics, for example, IELTS (International English Language Testing System) and NETEM (National Entrance Test of English for MA/MS Candidates). Hence, the ability to describe statistics presented in different forms is a basic skill of English writing and scientific research.

Also, in NETEM, the writing section will present a picture or cartoon, which reflects some social issue and requires the description and interpretation of the cartoon.

7.1 Figure and Chart Description

7.1.1 Different types of charts

7.1.1.1 Table

A table is a set of facts and figures arranged in columns and rows.

Sample 7-1-1-1-1

Changes in people's diet

Food \ Year	1986	1987	1988	1989	1990
Grain	49%	47%	46.5%	45%	45%
Milk	10%	11%	11%	12%	13%

continued

Food \ Year	1986	1987	1988	1989	1990
Meat	17%	20%	22.5%	23%	21%
Fruit and Vegetables	24%	22%	20%	20%	21%
Total	100%	100%	100%	100%	100%

7.1.1.2　Chart

A chart is a diagram that makes information easier to understand by showing how two or more sets of data are related. There are two common types of chart, a pie chart and a bar chart.

Pie chart—A pie chart is a circle divided into segments. It is usually used to show percentages.

Sample 7-1-1-2-1

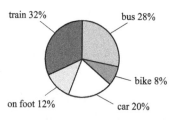

Travelling commuters

Bar chart—A bar chart is a diagram that makes information easier to understand by showing how two or more sets of data are related.

Sample 7-1-1-2-2

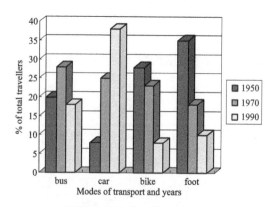

Different modes of transport

7.1.1.3　Graph

A graph is a diagram, usually a line or curve, which shows how two or more sets of numbers or measurements are related. Line graphs compare two variables. Each variable is plotted along an axis. A line graph has a vertical axis and a horizontal axis. Usually, there are three types of graphs—single-line graph, two-line graph and three-line graph.

Sample 7-1-1-3-1: Single-line graph

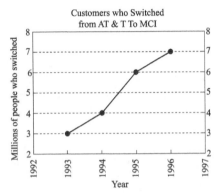

Customers who switched from AT&T to MCI

Sample 7-1-1-3-2: Two-line graph

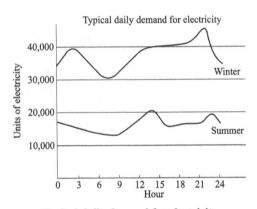

Typical daily demand for electricity

Sample 7-1-1-3-3: Three-line graph

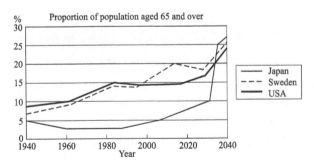

Proportion of population aged 65 and over

7.1.1.4　Flow chart

A flowchart is a type of diagram that represents an algorithm, workflow or process, showing the steps as boxes of various kinds and their order by connecting them with arrows.

Sample 7-1-1-4-1

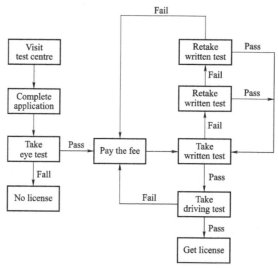

Process of getting a driving license

Sometimes, different types of charts are used together in the test, for example, the combination of two pie charts, the combination of pie chart and bar chart or the combination of pie chart and graph, etc.

Sample 7-1-1-4-2

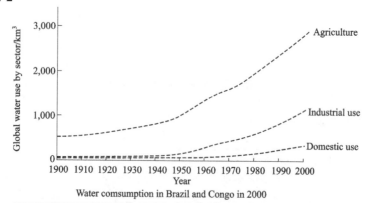

Water consumption

7.1.2 Useful words and phrases to describe graphs

7.1.2.1 Useful verbs and nouns to show trends

VERB		NOUN	
UP	**DOWN**	**UP**	**DOWN**
increase	decrease	increase	decrease
go up	go down	rise	reduction
rise	decline	growth	decline
grow	fall	jump	fall
jump	drop	surge	drop
climb	shrink	upturn	downturn
shoot up	slide	upward trend	downturn trend
surge	dip		
soar	collapse		
rocket	plummet		
ascend	descend		
pick up	dive		
mount	reduce		
edge up	edge down		
leap	diminish		
shoot	lessen		
	plunge		

7.1.2.2 Useful adjectives and adverbs to show degree and speed

DEGREES OF CHANGE		SPEED OF CHANGE	
Adjectives	Adverbs	Adjectives	Adverbs
dramatic	dramatically	abrupt	abruptly
sharp	sharply	sudden	suddenly
considerable	considerably	rapid	rapidly
significant	significantly	quick	quickly
substantial	substantially	steady	steadily
moderate	moderately	gradual	gradually
slight	slightly	slow	slowly
marginal	marginally		

7.1.2.3 Expressions for other features

NO CHANGE	TOP	BOTTOM
fluctuate	reach a peak	reach the bottom
stabilize	peak (v.)	reach a low point
level off / out	top out	bottom out
stay at the same level	hit the top / peak / the highest point / the all-time high	decline to / drop to the bottom
remain / maintain / stay / keep stable/ steady / constant / unchanged / fixed		

7.1.3 Useful sentence patterns to describe graphs

Introduction	1. As we can see from the chart / graph / table / diagram, … 2. The chart / graph / table / diagram shows / displays / indicates that… 3. As shown in / According to the chart / graph / table / diagram, … 4. The figures / statistics in the chart reflect / show / reveal that… 5. The chart / graph / table / diagram illustrates / describes / compares… 6. It is clear / apparent from the chart / graph / table / diagram that…
Percentage	1. …has the largest percentage / proportion of… 2. …accounts for / takes up 10%. 3. Compared with A, B has a higher percentage. 4. On the top of the list is …, which accounts for 60%. 5. At the bottom is …, which takes up 20%. 6. A is ranked / rated first, followed by B at 30% and C at 25%.
Increase / decrease	1. The number of private cars increased / rose suddenly / rapidly / dramatically / substantially / considerably / sharply / steeply from…to … 2. There was a sudden / rapid / dramatic / substantial / considerable / sharp / steep increase / rise in the number of private cars from…to… 3. There was a boom in the number of private cars from …to … 4. The number of private cars climbed / jumped/rose suddenly / went sharply up/soared to …in 2006. 5. There was an evident / apparent / obvious increase in purchasing private cars from… to… 6. The number of private cars increased / rose steadily / gradually from…to… 7. There was a steady / gradual increase / rise in the number of private cars from…to… 8. There was a slight / slow increase / rise in the number of private cars from …to… 9. The number of private cars decreased / fell / dropped suddenly / rapidly / dramatically / substantially / considerably / sharply / steeply from…to … 10. There was a sudden / rapid / dramatic / substantial / sharp / steep decrease / drop / reduction / decline in the number of private cars from…to… 11. The number of private cars increased / rose by …% from…to… 12. The number of private cars fell / dropped / declined by…% from…to… 13. The number of private cars dropped sharply / went sharply down to … in ….
Little difference	1. The number of private cars remained level / steady / stable / constant between … and … 2. The number of private cars stayed the same between…and… 3. The number of private cars appeared to level off. 4. There was little / hardly any change in the number of private cars between…and…

continued

Summit/ bottom	1. The situation / figures reached a peak / a height at …% in 2006. 2. The situation / figures bottomed out at …% in 2005. 3. The situation / figures peaked at …% in 2006. 4. The number soared to a record high of …
Multiplication	1. A is twice / three times / four times what it was in … 2. A is twice / three times / four times the amount in … 3. The figure doubled / tripled between …and… 4. The output of steel in 2006 was 400% up compared with that in 2002.

7.1.4 Basic structure of essays describing graphs

Generally, the basic structure of an essay describing graphs consists of three major elements.

(1) Describe the graph.

(2) Possible reasons for the phenomenon.

(3) Your comments.

However, it should be noted that the writing tasks of some exams may have different requirements. For example, in IELTS writing section, Task One requires only description of the statistics presented in the charts or graphs. No analysis of reason or comment is needed.

7.1.5 Samples

Sample 7-1-5-1

Writing section of NETEM in 1997.

Directions: *Study the following set of pictures carefully and write an essay in no less than 120 words. Your essay should cover all the information provided and meet the requirements below:*

1. Interpret the following pictures.

2. Predict the tendency of tobacco consumption and give your reasons.

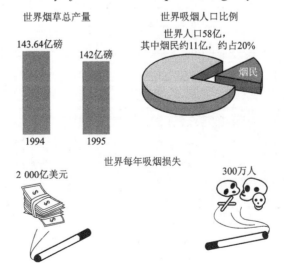

Sample essay:

As is shown in the bar chart, the total production of tobacco in the world shrank from 14.364 billion pounds in 1994 to 14.2 billion pounds in 1995. According to the figures given in the pie chart, tobacco consumers account for 20% of the world population. This causes great harm to us. Financially, it results in a yearly loss of 200 billion US dollars spent on cigarettes. Physically, about 3 million people on the globe die from smoking-related diseases every year.

Faced with such a threat, people from all walks of life have tried various measures for a total tobacco ban. For one thing, health experts try hard to warn the public of the dangers involved. For another, the authorities pass laws to limit tobacco production and consumption, raise tobacco taxes and prohibit smoking in public places. More importantly, the public launch campaigns to cut smoking.

On the basis of the analyses above, we can predict the future tendency confidently. With the further growth in economy and more changes in life style, the tendency of tobacco consumption indicated in the table will definitely decrease in the years to come. (190 words)

Highlights: *Financially*, it results in a yearly loss of 200 billion US dollars spent on cigarettes. *Physically*, about 3 million people on the globe die from smoking-related diseases every year. (parallel sentences starting with -ly)

Sample 7-1-5-2

Writing section of NETEM in 1999.

Directions: *Study the graphs carefully and write an essay in at least 150 words. Your essay should cover these three points:*

1. Effect of the country's growing human population on its wildlife.

2. Possible reasons for the effect.

3. Your suggestions for wildlife protection.

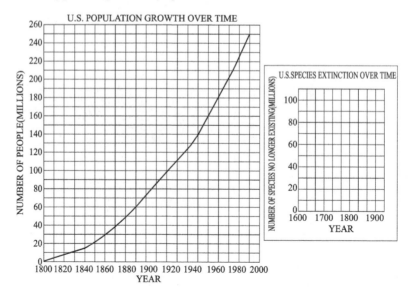

Sample essay:

　　As is shown by the two graphs, the U.S. population soared from 2 million to 250 million from 1800 to 1990. In contrast, the number of wildlife species no longer existing shot up, adding up to 70 over the same period of time. It is obvious that the increase in the U.S. population has been accompanied by a corresponding decline in the number of wildlife species. *Far too many species have been lost already, which poses a danger to the ecological balance.*

　　As the human population expands, more and more wild animals are hunted for food, or because they are thought to present a threat to man. But studies show that one of the primary causes of the disappearance of wildlife is pollution, which is one of the consequences of population growth and economic development. This makes us wonder if man is able to share this planet in harmony with other life forms.

　　In my opinion, it is imperative to take steps to reverse the disturbing trend illustrated in the charts. One measure would be to forbid the building of cities in areas where wild life is threatened with extinction. But, more importantly, man must learn to stop polluting the environment, or he himself will become extinct.

Highlights: ***Far too many species have been lost already****, which poses a danger to the ecological balance.* (a sentence/clause as the antecedent of which)

Sample 7-1-5-3

　　Writing Task One of IELTS.

Directions: *The table below summarizes some data collected by a college bookshop for the month of February 1995. Write a report describing the sales figures of various types of publications, based on the information shown in the table. You should write at least 150 words.*

Items	Non-Book Club Members			Book Club Members	Total
	College staff	College Students	Members of Public		
Fiction	44	31	—	76	151
Non-Fiction	29	194	122	942	1,287
Magazines	332	1,249	82	33	1,696
Total	405	1,474	204	1,051	3,134

Sample essay:

　　The table shows the sales figures of fiction books, non-fiction books and magazines in a college bookshop for February 1995. The figures are divided into two groups: sales to non-Book Club members and to Book Club members.

The non-Book Club member figures are comprised of sales to college staff, college students and members of the public. College staff bought 332 magazines, 44 fiction and 29 non-fiction books. College students bought 1,249 magazines, 194 non-fiction and 31 fiction books. More magazines were sold to college students than to other groups of customers. Although non-fiction books were sold to members of the public, they purchased 122 non-fiction books and 82 magazines.

Book Club members bought more fiction (76) and non-fiction books (942) than other customers. On the other hand, magazine sales to members (33) were fewer than the combined magazine sales to other customers.

The total number of publications sold for the month was 3,134 (1,474 to college students, 405 to college staff and 204 to members of the public). Of this figure, 151 items were fiction books and 1,287 were non-fiction. Therefore, magazines accounted for the greatest number of sales (1,696).

Highlights: *The table shows* the sales figures of fiction books, non-fiction books, and magazines in a college bookshop for February 1995. *The figures are divided into two groups:* sales to non-Book Club members and to Book Club members. (The opening paragraph clearly summarizes the contents of the table.)

Sample 7-1-5-4

Writing Task One of IELTS.

Directions: *The chart shows the different modes of transport used to travel to and from work in one European city in 1950, 1970 and 1990. Write a report for a university lecturer describing the information shown. You should write at least 150 words.*

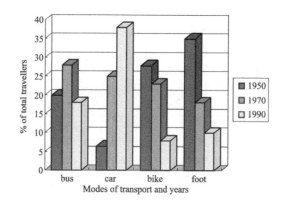

Sample essay:

The chart shows the percentage of travelers in a European city who used buses, cars, bikes and feet to commute to and from work in the years 1950, 1970 and 1990.

The most significant change occurred in the use of cars. The percentage of people driving cars grew considerably, rising from just over 5% in 1950 to 25% in 1970, and then climbing to almost 40%

by 1990. However, traveling by bike fell dramatically. Over 25% of commuters cycled in 1950, but this had fallen to less than 10% by 1990. Similarly, the proportion of people who walked to work fell from more than a third in 1950 to about 10% in 1990, while the percentage of people taking buses initially rose to about 30% in 1970, but dropped to about 17% in 1990.

The graph indicates the growing use of cars for commuting and the corresponding fall in the popularity of other modes of transport since 1950.

Highlights: *The percentage of people driving cars grew considerably, **rising** from just over 5% in 1950 to 25% in 1970...*(present participle as adverbial)

Sample 7-1-5-5

Writing Task One of IELTS.

Directions: *The three pie charts below show the changes in annual spending by a particular UK school in 1981, 1991 and 2001. Summarize the information by selecting and reporting the main features and make comparisons where relevant. Write at least 150 words.*

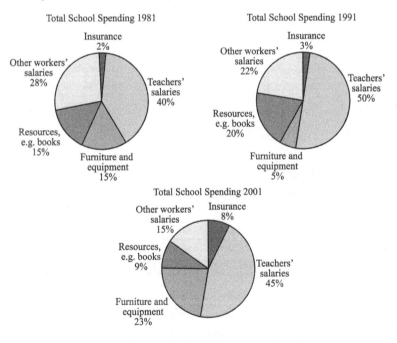

Sample essay:

The charts provided describe the changes in annual cost of UK school in the year of 1981, 1991 and 2001.

In detail, teachers' salaries occupied the largest percentage of the spending in the three years, and it peaked at 50% in 1991. Other workers' salaries accounted for the second largest percentage with 28% in 1981. But it decreased to 15% in the year of 2001. The spending of resources such as books had also declined to 9% after reaching a maximum of 20%. However, the percentage of insurance experienced a growth, from 2% in 1981 to 8% in 2001. The spending of furniture and equipment was fluctuating. Finally, it got the highest point of 23% in 2001 although the percentage of it reduced to 5% in 1991.

To conclude, the spending of teachers' salaries retained the biggest percentage. In addition, the percentage of insurance and furniture and equipment increased and others decreased.

Highlights: ... *occupied the largest percentage, peaked, accounted for the second largest percentage, decreased, declined, experienced a growth, fluctuating, got the highest point, reduced* ... (words and phrases describing the tendency)

Sample 7-1-5-6

Writing Task One of IELTS.

Directions: *The charts below give information about travel to and from the UK, and about the most popular countries for UK residents to visit. Summarize the information by selecting and reporting the main features and make comparisons where relevant. Write at least 150 words.*

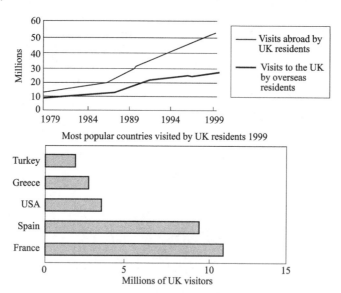

Sample essay:

The two graphs present the results of a survey into travel in the UK. The first one illustrates the number of UK residents traveling abroad and that of overseas residents traveling in the UK from 1979 to 1999. The second reveals the most popular destinations to UK tourists in 1999.

From the first line chart, we can see that the total numbers of both UK travelers and overseas travelers grew over the two decades. The figure of UK residents traveling abroad rose gradually from 13 million in 1979 to 20 million in 1986. After that, a significant increase occurred, with the total reaching 52 million in 1999. Similarly, the number of overseas tourists to the UK showed a steady *increase during the period, rising from 10 million to 26 million. In 1999, the number of UK travelers was twice that of overseas travelers coming to the UK.*

According to the second bar chart, France was the top travel destination with more than 11 million of UK visitors, followed by Spain with 9 million UK tourists. The other three popular destinations were USA, Greece and Turkey, with the figures of UK travelers reaching 4 million, 3 million and 2 million respectively. Obviously, West Europe was the first choice for UK residents.

Highlights: *After that, a significant increase occurred,* **with the total reaching ...** *(absolute construction—with + n.+ participle)*

Sample 7-1-5-7

Writing Task One of IELTS.

Directions: *The graph and table below give information about water use worldwide and water consumption in two different countries. Summarize the information by selecting and reporting the main features, and make comparisons where relevant. Write at least 150 words.*

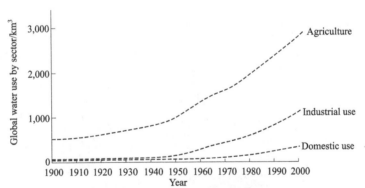

Water comsumption in Brazil and Congo in 2000

Country	Population	Irrigated land	Water consumption per person
Brazil	176 million	26,500 km²	359 m³
Democratic Republic of Congo	5.2 million	100 km²	8 m³

Sample essay:

The curve graph illustrates the global water consumption for different sectors, namely the agricultural, industrial and domestic sectors, from 1900 to 2000.

To be more specific, water used in the agricultural region rose dramatically throughout the century, from about 50 km³ in 1,900 to around 3,000 km³ in 2,000. Meanwhile, water consumption in the other two sectors also experienced a rising trend. It was not until mid-century that industrial and domestic spending of water started to grow. From 1950 onwards, industrial and domestic water uses grew steadily to over 1,000 km³ and 500 km³ respectively.

The table displays differences in water consumption between Brazil and Congo. Compared with the area of irrigated land of 26,500 km² in Brazil, Congo's land is obviously smaller at merely 100 km². Naturally, this implies that a high proportion of water is used for agricultural purposes in both countries, and the inference is also supported by the figures for water consumption per person: 359 m³ in Brazil and, in contrast, only 8 m³ in Congo.

In summary, agricultural usage of water is the largest among all sectors worldwide. The more irrigated land a country has, the more water it generally requires.

Highlights: ***In summary***, *agricultural usage...* ***The more*** *irrigated land a country has,* ***the more*** *water it generally requires.* (sentence pattern to summarize, and the use of comparative structure)

Sample 7-1-5-8

Writing Task One of IELTS.

Directions: *The diagrams below show the life cycle of the silkworm and the stages in the production of silk cloth. Summarize the information by selecting and reporting the main features, and make comparisons where relevant. Write at least 150 words.*

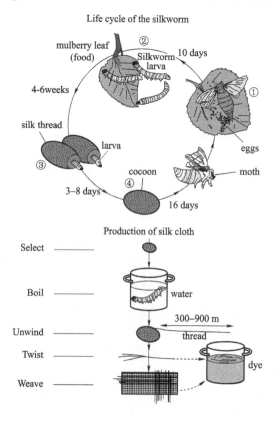

Sample essay:

The first diagram shows the life cycle of the silkworm that is divided into four stages. And the second illustrates the processing of cloth making in stages.

From the first diagram, initially, eggs are laid by the moth and it takes ten days for each egg to hatch out. Then the larva living on the mulberry leaves also feed on the leaves. Subsequently, after utmost six weeks, the larva spins silk threads to form a cocoon. After a period of around a week, in the fourth stage, the silk threads are rolled into a cocoon. Finally, sixteen days later, a moth emerges from the cocoon and the life cycle restarts once more.

From the second diagram, there are five main stages in the cloth making: selecting, boiling, unwinding, twisting and weaving (dying also included). Once selected, sounded cocoons are heated in hot water until they start to unwind. The ideal condition is that the thread can be between 300 and 900 meters long, which shall be twisted together for the weaving and dying stages at last.

Highlights: *initially; then; subsequently; in the fourth stage; finally.* (words to indicate order)

7.2 Cartoon Description

7.2.1 Basic structure of essays describing cartoons

Usually, such an essay consists of three major parts:

(1) Describe the drawing.

(2) Interpret the meaning.

(3) Your comments.

7.2.2 Useful expressions and sentence patterns

Describe the drawing	Interpret the meaning
1. As is shown/described in the picture, … 2. As is vividly depicted/ illustrated in the picture, … 3. The picture / drawing / cartoon vividly depicts … 4. What we see in this picture is…… 5. From the picture, we can see… 6. In this cartoon, … 7. The caption reads, "…"	1. The purpose of the drawing is to show us that… 2. The symbolic meaning subtly conveyed is that… 3. We can deduce from the cartoon that importance has to be attached to the issue of … 4. The picture aims at revealing a serious problem that… 5. It seems that the cartoonist is sending a message about the significance of … 6. Obviously, the cartoon is meant to draw our attention to the phenomenon of … 7. Undoubtedly, the drawer is trying to attract our attention to the tragedy of … 8. What the picture conveys goes far beyond only a … Instead, it … 9. This simple picture is a wake-up call to everyone. 10. The implication of this thought-provoking drawing should be taken seriously.

Your comments		
1. To overcome this difficulty, it is essential for us to take steps to reverse the disturbing trend illustrated in the cartoon. 2. The issue calls for immediate action from… 3. One measure would be… But more importantly,… 4. I believe our joint efforts will eventually pay off and a happy and bright future is awaiting us.	5. In view of the seriousness of this problem, effective measures should be taken before things get worse. 6. For one thing, we need to launch a publicizing campaign for/against… For another, we should urge the authorities to put an end to… 7. Only in this way can we succeed in the fight against…	8. Obviously, the situation of … will eventually get out of hand unless effective measures are taken. 9. On (the) one hand, awareness of … is a prerequisite for the solution to the problem. On the other, relevant laws and regulations should be made to… 10. Only by doing so can we have a harmonious society.

7.2.3 Samples

Sample 7-2-3-1

Writing section of NETEM in 2006.

Directions: *Study the following photos carefully and write an essay of 160-200 words in which you should*

　　1. describe the photos briefly;

　　2. interpret the social phenomenon reflected by them; and

　　3. give your point of view.

把崇拜写在脸上　　　　花 300 元做个小贝头

注：Beckham 是英国足球明星

Sample essay:

　　It goes without saying that the pictures reflect a common and serious problem in China—worship of celebrities among young people. In the left hand picture, a man has had David Beckham's name written on his face. In the right hand picture, a man who is having a haircut asks his barber to cut his hair on the model of David Beckham, the popular British soccer star.

　　It is not uncommon for Chinese young people to have super stars as their idols. Most of them are fans of certain basketball players, football players, singers, actors and actresses at home and abroad. These fans not only watch the matches, TV serials and movies starring their heroes, but also pay a large sum of money to gain access to a live show, a concert, and so on. Moreover, they imitate their idols in almost every aspect of their lives, such as their hair styles, glasses and clothes.

PART TWO COMPOSING ESSAYS

There is nothing wrong for one to have his own role model. Unfortunately, if people adore the pop stars to the extent of losing self-control, they misunderstand the significance of popular culture. Anyway, popular culture is to enrich our life. Young people should learn how to live their own lives instead of blindly following others' footsteps.

Highlights: *It is **not uncommon** for Chinese young people to have super stars as their idols.* (double negative for emphasis)

Sample 7-2-3-2
    Writing section of NETEM in 2010.
Directions: *Write an essay of 160-200 words based on the following drawing. In your essay, you should*
    1. describe the drawing briefly;
    2. explain its intended meaning; and then
    3. give your comments.

文化"火锅"，既美味又营养

Sample essay:
    The cartoonist laid out the image elaborately, placing a steaming hotpot—the symbol of "integration"—at the center of the picture. What is conspicuous is that cultural ingredients in the pot are in great variety, ranging from domestic ones to overseas ones, from ancient to modern, from artistic to philosophic.
    Obviously, through this work, the cartoonist reveals us a truth: cultural diversity, in this integrated world, offers people more spiritual nutrition and quality life. In a culturally integrated age, people have more opportunities to broaden their horizon and enjoy a life open to the whole world. It is nothing unusual to see American writers attracted by Chinese glorious history or European physicians indulged in traditional Chinese medical science. Equally, it is not uncommon that some

Chinese designers frequently go to Milan or Florence for inspiration.

As the modern college students, we are bound to be beneficiaries of this trend and are accountable for promoting the exchange and combination of various cultures. While embracing the trend of cultural diversity, we have the duty to inherit the essences of our own culture and spread it to the whole world.

Highlights: ***The cartoonist laid out the image elaborately, placing*** *a steaming hotpot—the symbol of "integration"—**at the center of the picture**.*
What is conspicuous is that…
Obviously, through this work, the cartoonist reveals us a truth.
(good sentence patterns)

Sample 7-2-3-3

Directions: *Study the following drawing carefully and write an essay in which you should*

    1. describe the drawing;

    2. interpret its meaning; and

    3. suggest counter-measures.

学生的任务不仅仅是在学习上取满分

Sample essay:

As is vividly portrayed in the drawing above, a student is taking great pains to reach his destination—full score of school subjects like English, maths, physics and Chinese, neglecting such essential aspects as psychological/mental growth and moral standards. By his side, his teachers and parents are cheering him on. This drawing mirrors a common social phenomenon, which has aroused growing concern in contemporary society.

The message conveyed by the picture is that too much attention and efforts have been directed towards children's academic performances rather than the development of personality and establishment of morals. According to some teachers and parents, academic achievement is another name for success. Unfortunately, the fact that some students in famous universities suffering from psychological problems commit suicide suggests that they sometimes lack the confidence and courage to face the ups and downs in life. Therefore, more thought needs to be given to the proper education we desire.

In order for students to survive the fierce competition in modern world, their psychological well-being and values deserve due attention from schools and families. The transition from exam-oriented education system to all-round development has been the first step in the right direction. More importantly, concern in this regard from parents as well as teachers is advisable, which can not only ensure a happy and healthy generation, but also contribute to a harmonious society.

Highlights: *Unfortunately,* ***the fact that****...suggests that... (appositive clause)*

Sample 7-2-3-4

Writing section of NETEM in 2013.

Directions: *Study the following drawing carefully and write an essay to*

    1. describe the drawing briefly;

    2. explain its intended meaning; and

    3. give your comments.

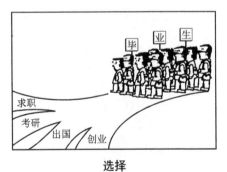

选择

Sample essay:

Have you ever been caught in a dilemma? If so, you may feel the same awkwardness as the graduates in the picture do. In the drawing, facing several choices, including hunting for an ideal job, going abroad, achieving future education or starting their own business, they cease their steps, feeling puzzled and wondering where to go.

Conceived in the inspirational cartoon is a simple truth that one should make sensible choices and, more importantly, adhere to the decisions. Indeed, decision-making on graduating will have some influence on one's life. So he should take into consideration of different features of each option, *personality traits and economic status so that he can make an advisable choice. Moreover, once coming to a decision, one should do his utmost to achieve the goal, which requires hard-work, patience and perseverance.*

As a college student, I was confronted with such a cross road several months ago. With the reminding from friends—"education is the access to opportunities"—I chose to take the National Entrance Examination for Postgraduates. With this decision, I am determined to head on without any hesitation.

Highlights: *Have you ever been caught in a dilemma? If so, you may feel the same awkwardness as the graduates in the picture do.*
Conceived in the inspirational cartoon is a simple truth that *one should...*
(good sentence patterns)

Sample 7-2-3-5

Writing section of NETEM in 2012.

Directions: *Write an essay of 160-200 words based on the following drawing. In your essay, you should*

1. describe the drawing briefly;
2. explain its intended meaning; and then
3. give your comments.

Sample essay:

As is portrayed in this cartoon, two men express different attitudes toward a fallen bottle with liquor spilling out. Standing there depressed, one of them is lamenting, "It is all over!" At the same time, the other is cheering, "It is so lucky that there is still some left." What do their distinctly different reactions stand for? Of course, pessimism and optimism!

Through this unique metaphor, the writer of the cartoon intends to tell us that different attitudes may lead to totally different results. Optimistic people can always discover positive sides, while pessimistic guys keep complaining and giving up, with endless losses. Here is a story. Two salesmen went to sell shoes in an African town only to find natives never have shoes on. One salesman sadly *gave up but the other, cheerfully, spent months showing natives the benefit of shoes. Obviously, the latter won the full market share.*

What's the point? The point is that "we should never cry over spilt milk, but make the best out of the rest!" That is, only with that positive view on difficulties or frustrations can we deal with them with hope, with joy and with fruitful rewards.

Highlights: *As is portrayed in this cartoon, …*
What do their distinctly different reactions stand for?
What's the point? The point is …
(good sentence patterns)

Sample 7-2-3-6

Directions: *Write an essay of 160-200 words based on the following drawing. In your essay, you should*
  1. *describe the drawing briefly;*
  2. *explain its intended meaning; and then*
  3. *give your comments.*

Sample essay:
As is implied in the picture, a new trend in higher education is the retreat from humanities to science and technology and other career-oriented disciplines. In universities, there has been an increasing expansion of departments such as finance, law, accounting, management, and so on. Even candidates for colleges and universities become more and more practically-minded when it comes to the choice of majors. Throughout the country, schools are under pressure to become more vocationalized.

One reason is that it is difficult to get grants for the liberal arts studies, for, unlike the specialized studies whose results can be immediately converted into profits, what the liberal arts studies produce is only helpful to the nurturing of ethics and human values. The second is that parents and students tend to devalue the majors that are less appealing to employers in a rapidly tightening job market. As a result, literature and philosophy are only regarded as intellectual nourishment, contributing nothing directly to a job.

However, the goal of education is to produce not only specialists, but also educated and developed mind because being productive requires not only professional capabilities, but also the ability to confront the world with grace and the ability to create the joy of living. So instead of making the liberal arts shrink, it is time for us to find ways to infuse them into other specialized studies. Only by doing so can we produce the well-developed talents for the future.

Highlights: *career-oriented, practically-minded, well-developed.*
(compound adjectives)

PART THREE
WRITING FOR PRACTICAL PURPOSES

Introduction

This part includes several chapters on practical writing such as personal letter writing (letters of invitation, letters of thanks, letters of condolence, letters of congratulations) and correspondence writing, applying for university admission, employment writing, notes and memos writing, notices and posters writing, etc.

Chapter Eight

Personal Letters and Social Correspondences

Introduction

Personal letters are important means of communication, written between family members, friends, colleagues and acquaintances about everyday affairs. They are representatives of the writer's personality. Usually, people write personal letters to express thanks for the kindness of someone, congratulate someone on something good that happened to him or her, accept or refuse something offered to them, transmit news and greetings to others, issue invitations, and sometimes, send apologies, sympathies and condolences as well. Chapter Eight will introduce the format of letter writing and letters used for different practical purposes, for example, letters of invitation, thanks, condolences and congratulations.

8.1 Format and Envelope of a Letter

8.1.1 Format of a letter

Business letters or personal letters normally have **seven parts**: the heading, date, inside address, greeting or salutation, body, complimentary close and signature line.

1. The heading

This includes the address, line by line, with the last line being the date. Skip a line after the heading. If using preaddressed stationery called letterhead, just add the date.

2. The date line

The date on which the letter is written. Remember that the month in letters is preferred because figures may create confusion.

3. The inside address

The inside address is the recipient's address.

4. The greeting or salutation

The greeting usually ends with a comma. The greeting may be formal, beginning with the word "dear" and the addressee's given name or relationship, or it may be informal if appropriate.

Formal: Dear Uncle Jim,/Dear Mr. Wilkins,

Informal: Hi Joe,/Greetings,

[Occasionally very personal greetings may end with an exclamation mark ("!") for emphasis.]

5. The body

Also known as the main text. This includes the message you want to write. Skip a space between paragraphs. Skip a line after the greeting and before the close.

6. The complimentary close

This short expression is always a few words in a single line. It ends in a comma. Skip one to three spaces (two is usual) for the signature line.

7. The signature line

Type or print your name. The handwritten signature goes above this line and below the close. The signature should be written in blue or black ink. If the letter is quite informal, you may omit the signature line as long as you sign the letter.

8. The optional parts

1) Attain line

It is used when a writer of a letter attached to an organization wishes to direct the letter to a particular person who is in charge of the business. Attain line is put two lines above the greeting.

e.g. Attain: Mr. John Smith

For the Attain of Mr. John Smith

2) Subject line

It is often between the greeting and the body of the letter to call attention to the topic of the letter.

e.g.   Subject: Contract No. 111988

3) Enclosure

A document or object placed in an envelope together with a letter. If something is enclosed, note it in the letter two lines below the signature.

e.g. Enclosure: 2 copies of Contract

Enc.: Price List

Leave a margin on each side of the paper—about two centimeters at the top and a centimeter at the other three sides of the page.

There are mainly four popular styles of business letters or personal letters: **block style, modified block style, semi-block style** and **modified semi-block style**.

Block style: Align all elements on the left margin.

[SENDER'S FULL NAME AND TITLE]
[SENDER'S COMPANY NAME]
[SENDER'S ADDRESS]
[SENDER'S PHONE]
[SENDER'S E-MAIL]

[DATE]

[RECIPIENT'S FULL NAME]
[RECIPIENT'S COMPANY]
[RECIPIENT'S ADDRESS]

ATTAIN:

Dear [RECIPIENT],

Subject:

[BODY]
Xxxxxxxxxxxxxxxxxxxxxxxxxxxxxxxxxxxxxxxxxxxxxxxxxxxxxxxxxxx
xxxxxxxxxxxxxxxxxxxxxxxxxxxxxxxxxxxxxxxxxxxxxxxxxxxxxxxxx.

Xxxxxxxxxxxxxxxxxxxxxxxxxxxxxxxxxxxxxxxxxxxxxxxxxxxxxxxxxxx
xxxxxxxxxxxxxxxxxxxxxxxxxxxxxxxxxxxxxxxxxxxxxxxxxxxxxxxxx.

[COMPLIMENTARY CLOSING]
[SENDER'S FULL NAME]
[SENDER'S TITLE]

Enclosures: (number of enclosures)

Semi-block Style: All elements are aligned to the left margin except for the body of the letter. The first sentence of each paragraph is indented, usually leaving a space of four or five letters.

[SENDER'S FULL NAME AND TITLE]
[SENDER'S COMPANY NAME]
[SENDER'S ADDRESS]
[SENDER'S PHONE]
[SENDER'S E-MAIL]

[DATE]

[RECIPIENT'S FULL NAME]
[RECIPIENT'S COMPANY]
[RECIPIENT'S ADDRESS]

Dear [RECIPIENT],

[BODY]
    Xxxxxxxxxxxxxxxxxxxxxxxxxxxxxxxxxxxxxxxxxxxxxxxxx
xxxxxxxxxxxxxxxxxxxxxxxxxxxxxxxxxxxxxxxxxxxxxxxxxxxxxxxxx
xxxxxxxxxxx.

    Xxxxxxxxxxxxxxxxxxxxxxxxxxxxxxxxxxxxxxxxxxxxxxxxx
xxxxxxxxxxxxxxxxxxxxxxxxxxxxxxxxxxxxxxxxxxxxxxxxxxxxxxxxx
xxxxxxxxxxx.

[COMPLIMENTARY CLOSING]
[SENDER'S FULL NAME]
[SENDER'S TITLE]

Enclosures: (number of enclosures)

Modified Block Style: All text is aligned to the left margin, except for the inside address, date and closing, and paragraphs are not indented. The inside address, date and closing usually begin at the center point.

[SENDER'S FULL NAME AND TITLE]
[SENDER'S COMPANY NAME]
[SENDER'S ADDRESS]
[SENDER'S PHONE]
[SENDER'S E-MAIL]

[DATE]

[RECIPIENT'S FULL NAME]
[RECIPIENT'S COMPANY]
[RECIPIENT'S ADDRESS]

ATTAIN:

Dear [RECIPIENT],

Subject:

[BODY]
Xxxxxxxxxxxxxxxxxxxxxxxxxxxxxxxxxxxxxxxxxxxxxxxxxxxx
xxxxxxxxxxxxxxxxxxxxxxxxxxxxxxxxxxxxxxxxxxxxxxxxx.

Xxxxxxxxxxxxxxxxxxxxxxxxxxxxxxxxxxxxxxxxxxxxxxxxxxxx
xxxxxxxxxxxxxxxxxxxxxxxxxxxxxxxxxxxxxxxxxxxxxxxxx.

[COMPLIMENTARY CLOSING]
[SENDER'S FULL NAME]
[SENDER'S TITLE]

Enclosures: (number of enclosures)

Modified Semi-block Style: All text is aligned to the left margin, except for the inside address, date and closing, and the first sentence of each paragraph is indented.

[SENDER'S FULL NAME AND TITLE]
[SENDER'S COMPANY NAME]
[SENDER'S ADDRESS]
[SENDER'S PHONE]
[SENDER'S E-MAIL]

[DATE]

[RECIPIENT'S FULL NAME]
[RECIPIENT'S COMPANY]
[RECIPIENT'S ADDRESS]

ATTAIN:

Dear [RECIPIENT],

Subject:

[BODY]
  Xxxxxxxxxxxxxxxxxxxxxxxxxxxxxxxxxxxxxxxxxxxxxx
xxxxxxxxxxxxxxxxxxxxxxxxxxxxxxxxxxxxxxxxxxxxxxxxxxx.

  Xxxxxxxxxxxxxxxxxxxxxxxxxxxxxxxxxxxxxxxxxxxxxx
xxxxxxxxxxxxxxxxxxxxxxxxxxxxxxxxxxxxxxxxxxxxxxxxxxx.

[COMPLIMENTARY CLOSING]
[SENDER'S FULL NAME]
[SENDER'S TITLE]

Enclosures: (number of enclosures)

8.1.2 Format of an envelope

  The envelope should be a standard size that matches the stationery (approximately 4" × 9½" for standard 8½" × 11" stationery). Fold the letter twice so that it is creased to make thirds. This will fit easily in a standard envelope and it is easy to unfold.

  The following picture shows what one envelope should be like. The horizontal lines represent lines of type.

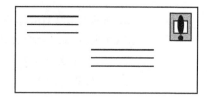

The information on the envelope normally contains **two parts** besides the stamp which is on the right top corner of the envelope.

(1) The ***address of the recipient*** is in the middle of the envelope, beginning approximately halfway down. (Make sure most of it is below the stamp, or it may get covered over by the cancellation.)

(2) The ***return address*** usually locates in the upper left corner. It is not necessary to type it in if the stationery is preprinted with the return address.

Tips:
- If you are using business envelopes with a window (often transparent plastic), fold the letter so that the inside address can be seen through the window.
- Sometimes you can write your address on the reverse side of the envelope, i.e. on the flap.

Due to variations in stationery size, it may be necessary to fold a personal letter differently to fit in the envelope that matches the stationery.

If the personal letter is in a small envelope, the return address may be written on the envelope flap after the envelope is sealed.

```
Li Mingxin
Dept. of English
Beijing Foreign Studies Univ.           stamp
Beijing, 100081
China
            Prof. Richard Miller
            502 North Olive Avenue
            West Palm Beach, Florida 33402
            U.S.A.
```

How to Fold a Standard Letter

As stated in the section on envelopes, a letter, especially a business letter, is folded twice into horizontal thirds and placed into an envelope.

This insures a little privacy in the letter. The letter is also easy to unfold after the envelope is opened.

The following diagram shows how a letter is normally folded.

This type of folding is used regardless of letter style.

If the letter needs to have the address face out an envelope window, make the second fold in the same location but opposite direction. The letter will then be folded in a **Z** shape and the address can be positioned to face out the window of the envelope.

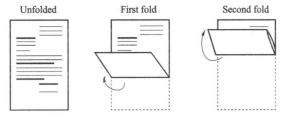

Unfolded   First fold   Second fold

Ex. 8-1-1

Directions: *Write a letter to your friend and tell him or her about your new life on campus, envelope included.*

8.2 Invitation Letter

8.2.1 What are included in a letter of invitation?

A letter of invitation often includes:

- Who will be invited to attend what kind of activity for what purpose.
- The time, place and other details of the activity arrangement.
- The inquiry for the recipient to clarify if he or she will accept the invitation before certain time, if necessary.

Tips:

Make sure to include when necessary:
- Name of the person sponsoring the event(who is the host/hostess).
- Exactly who is invited (can someone bring a guest, spouse).
- What type of social event is being held.
- Directions or a map if the location is difficult to find.
- The phone number and deadline to reply; precede these facts with "R.S.V.P" (French for please reply).

8.2.2　Proper response to an invitation

If you can accept the invitation, express your pleasure and appreciation for it and confirm the time, date and place of the activity.

If you cannot accept the invitation, first express your appreciation for the invitation, and then your regret and give some reasons (concrete explanation is not needed, usually previous engagement or busy schedule) and send your regards at last.

Sample 8-2-2-1: Invitation to a formal dinner

Dear Mr. White,

　　To celebrate the 20th anniversary of Guangzhou Trading Co. Ltd, we are holding a dinner party at the Garden Hotel in Guangzhou from 7:00 to 10:00 p.m., on Friday, August 8.

　　You are cordially invited to the party so that we can express our sincere appreciation to you for the generous support you have extended to us for many years. For your information, the party will be attended by many top executives of leading Chinese and foreign trading companies, and we believe that this will offer many of us an excellent opportunity to get acquainted with each other.

　　We would be pleased to have your reply by July 15th so as to finalize our arrangements. We do hope that you will be able to join us in the occasion and look forward to seeing you at the party.

　　　　　　　　　　　　　　　　　　　　　　Sincerely yours,
　　　　　　　　　　　　　　　　　　　　　　Li Ming
　　　　　　　　　　　　　　　　　　　　　　Chairman of Guangzhou Trading Co. Ltd

Sample 8-2-2-2: Accepting an invitation

Dear Mr. Li,

　　I'd be delighted to attend the dinner party on Friday, August 8, at 7:00 p.m. at the Garden Hotel in Guangzhou. Thank you so much for inviting me. I'm looking forward to seeing you at the party.

　　　　　　　　　　　　　　　　　　　　　　Faithfully yours,
　　　　　　　　　　　　　　　　　　　　　　Paul White

Sample 8-2-2-3: Declining an invitation

Dear Mr. Yang,

　　Thank you for the invitation to the dinner party on Friday, August 8, celebrating the 20th anniversary of your esteemed company. Unfortunately, I'll be out of town on business on that day, so I won't be able to attend.

　　I'm very sorry, but please accept my thanks again for thinking of inviting me. I hope the evening will be a great success.

　　　　　　　　　　　　　　　　　　　　　　Faithfully yours,

Sample 8-2-2-4: Invitation to giving a lecture

Dear Dr. Smith,

All the staff of Guangzhou Trading Co., Ltd, have long admired your excellent research activities and would enjoy learning more about your work.

We would like to invite you to speak at the opening session of our annual seminar on Sales Promotion to be held at White Cloud Hotel on August 10th at 1:00 a. m.

Since this seminar runs sixty minutes, a fifty-minute address followed by a ten-minute question and answer period would be ideal.

About fifty persons are expected to attend, most of them being sales managers and others with backgrounds in marketing.

We do hope you can join us on August 10th.

I would appreciate having your reply by August 8th so that we can finalize our program.

Sincerely,

8.2.3 Useful phrases for personal invitation

Invitation:

(1) I'd like to invite you to our wedding ceremony.

(2) It would be very nice if you and your wife could come and spend the weekend 7th-8th June with us.

(3) We shall be glad if you will join us at a quiet dinner at Guangzhou Hotel next Friday evening at 7:00.

(4) I hope you will give me the pleasure of your company on the occasion of a dinner with a few friends next Saturday, the 12th, at 8 p.m.

(5). This is your official invitation to attend a fashion parade to launch Prada's Spring Collection for 2002.

(6) We are planning to celebrate the tenth business year of our company in China and shall be honored to have you as our guest, if you can manage it.

Acceptance:

(1) I would be delighted to come.

(2) Thank you so much. I'll surely come.

(3) Terrific! Nothing can prevent me. I'll be there on time.

(4) It is with great pleasure that we shall come to your wedding at that time.

(5) Nothing could give us more pleasure than accepting your kind invitation.

Refusal:

(1) What a pity! I accepted another invitation for that day.

(2) I'm sorry I can't accept your very kind invitation to tea party next Monday because I have another engagement on that day.

(3) Please accept my sincere regrets for not being able to join you at your birthday party.

(4) Unfortunately, the pressure of urgent business will not allow me to be present on this festive occasion.

Ex. 8-2-1

1. Invite your best friend to attend your wedding.

2. Your school invites a famous athlete to give a lecture on his or her successful career.

3. Your class is sponsoring the School Olympics. Write an invitation letter to ask other classes to participate in the event.

Tips:

- Before you write the invitation, plan the event. Will it be during the school day? After school? On the weekend? What games will it include? (Try to think of games that will involve everyone, not just the most athletic.) Will the event include food or other entertainment?
- Use words that will make people eager to come. Show that the event will be exciting and there will be a lot of fun to participate in it.
- Be sure to include important information, such as when and where the event will take place.
- Let participants know if there is anything they need to bring, such as sporting equipment or a snack lunch, or if a potluck is welcome.

8.3 Thank-you Letter

In some cases, a thank-you note is a must. In other cases, it's not required, but it's still a very good move. Wedding, Graduation, etc. do require a thank-you note be sent within 30 days of the event.

Thank-you letters may include the following information:

- Your appreciation for the gift, help, concern, invitation and so on.
- Words expressing the helpfulness of the gift, help, concern, invitation and so on.
- Thanks, best wishes and so on.

Tips:

- Be sincere (most people can detect whether you are sincere or not).
- Stick to the point.
- Write the thank-you letter as soon as possible after the event. For example, as for a job interview, this should be within 24 hours of the interview. However, it is not customary to thank the person beforehand.

- Use quality paper. Handwrite personal letters and use customized letterhead for business correspondence. E-mail may also be appropriate in less formal situations.
- Address your letter to a specific person, if possible, not just the company or organization in general.

Sample 8-3-1: Letter of Thanks for a sweater

Dear Aunt Jane,

Thank you so much for the sweater. It is so soft that I feel like you've sent me 100 hugs. When the weather gets colder, I'll definitely have you in my thoughts.

Thanks for your kindness.

Jane

Sample 8-3-2: Letter of Thanks for a tapestry

Dear Mr. Green,

Thank you most sincerely for your special gift of silk embroidered tapestry. We are greatly obliged to you not only for your gift but also for your kind thoughts that inspired it.

The gift is exactly what we most needed. It is hanging up on the wall of the meeting room of our company, and is admired by every visitor.

You are sincerely welcome to the opening ceremony of our company on 1 August, and then you would see how beautiful it looks there. Enclosed is our official invitation card for the opening ceremony.

Thank you again and look forward to seeing you then.

Yours sincerely,
Lin Jie
Manager of Public Relations
Guangzhou Trading Co., Ltd

Sample 8-3-3: Letter of Thanks for speech

Dear Mr. White,

Thanks for your help in making the meeting a great success.

Your presentation was so insightful that it generated a keen debate concerning the future development of the international trade. I'm certain the members have benefited greatly from your speech.

Once again, thank you for participating so effectively in the meeting and for playing a key role in making it a successful one.

Sincerely,
Mary Lee

Sample 8-3-4: Letter of Thanks for support from customers

Dear Mr. Brown,

  On July 6, Golden Star will celebrate its fifth anniversary. It's a wonderful occasion for us. And we're naturally a bit proud of the progress we've made in such a short time.

  Yet, we're fully aware that our accomplishments are not simply attributable to "genius" leadership or hard-working employees. We grew and prospered only because we found great friends like you who have given such loyal support along the way.

  So this is a thank-you note—for buying and pushing Golden Star products, putting up with occasional errors due to "growing pains," and just helping to put Golden Star on the map. The future looks bright, and we want to acknowledge your contribution to this rosy outlook. Thanks again.

Very sincerely yours,

James Green

President

Useful phrases for Letters of Thanks

(1) Thank you very much (very, very much; ever so much; most sincerely; indeed; from the bottom of my heart).

(2) Many thanks for your kind and warm letter.

(3) Thanks a million (ever so much).

(4) Please accept (I wish to express) my sincere (grateful; profound) appreciation for ...

(5) I sincerely (deeply; warmly) appreciate ...

(6) I am very (sincerely; most; truly) grateful to you for ...

(7) There is nothing more important (satisfying; grateful) to me than to receive one of your letters.

(8) Your letters are so much fun (comfort; entertainment; company).

(9) Your most courteous (considerate; delightful) letter...

Ex. 8-3-1

Directions: *You've received ____ (one book, CD, help, etc.) from your ____ (parents, friend, etc.) recently. Write a short note to thank them.*

8.4 Letter of Condolence and Consolation

8.4.1 The purpose of writing letters of condolence

  One of the most meaningful acts of kindness you can do for a mourner is to write a letter of condolence. The words of sympathy and memory are comforting to the bereaved. More importantly, mourners are very appreciative that you take the time to sit and compose a personal message to them or share a memory of the deceased. Mourners often save these letters for years.

Yet, the apparently simple act of writing a condolence letter is a lost art. Actually, letter-writing itself is a skill in danger of extinction, given the ease of calling on the phone. Of course, you can purchase commercially available condolence cards and add your own brief message, but a well-crafted personal letter of condolence is a wonderful gift to a mourner.

A good condolence letter has two goals: to offer tribute to the deceased and to be a source of comfort to the survivors. The best letters are like conversations on paper-free-flowing as if you were talking during a visit. Most often, they are written to the bereaved person to whom you feel closest, although it could be a general letter to the family. It should be written and sent promptly, generally within two weeks after the death. Use any standard stationery and write it by hand. Some etiquette experts recommend brevity, although if you have particular stories you wish to tell about the deceased, the letter may be lengthy.

The following are some specific guidelines for writing a good condolence letter.

(1) **Acknowledge the loss and name of the deceased.** This sets the purpose and tone of the letter. Let the bereaved know how you learned of the death and how you felt upon hearing the news. Using the name of the deceased is a tribute that comforts most mourners.

(2) **Express your sympathy.** Let the bereaved know your sadness. Use words of sympathy that share your own sorrow. This will remind the bereaved they are not alone in their suffering.

(3) **Note special qualities of the deceased.** Acknowledge those characteristics that you cherished most about the person who has died. These might be qualities of personality (leadership, sensitivity), or attributes (funny, good at sports), or ways the person related to the world (religious, devoted to community welfare). You might write of the special relationship you noted between the deceased and the bereaved.

(4) **Recall a memory about the deceased.** Tell a brief story or an anecdote that features the deceased. Try to capture what it was about the person in the story that you admired, appreciated or respected. Talk about how the deceased touched your life. Use humor—the funny stories are often the most appreciated by the bereaved.

(5) **Remind the bereaved of their personal strengths.** Bereavement often brings with it self-doubt and anxiety about one's own personal worth. By reminding the bereaved of the qualities they possess that will help them through this period, you reinforce their ability to cope. Among these qualities might be patience, optimism, religious belief, resilience, competence and trust. If you can recall something the deceased used to say about the mourner in this regard, you will really be giving your friend a gift.

(6) **Offer help, but be specific.** "If there is anything I can do, please call" actually puts a burden on those in grief who may be totally at a loss about what needs to be done. A definite offer to help with shopping, the kids, volunteer work or whatever is more appreciated. Then, do it—don't make

an offer you can't fulfill.

(7) **End with a word or phrase of sympathy.** Somehow, "sincerely," "love" or "fondly" don't quite make it. Try one of these: *"You are in my thoughts and prayers." "Our love is with you always." "We share in your grief and send you our love." "My affectionate respects to you and yours."*

Useful phrases for expressing condolences

(1) Please accept my love and sympathy.

(2) Please accept my deep condolences and heartfelt sympathy on the untimely passing away of Mr. Smith from illness.

(3) We are stunned by the tragic news.

(4) We sent our love and our deepest sympathy to you.

(5) On behalf of my colleagues and myself, I am writing to send you our most sincere condolences on the sad occasion of the death of your general manager.

(6) My regret and sorrow are beyond expression at this sad event.

(7) But for the sake of your health, we pray you not to oversorrow yourself.

(8) We had a genuine love and respect for him.

(9) May his soul rest in peace.

Sample 8-4-1-1: Expressing condolences on the death of a friend's mother

Dear Mike,

I wanted you to know that when I heard about the death of your Mother I was so saddened. She always had such a great smile every time I saw her. And her canned raspberry-peach jam was the best I've ever tasted. I will miss her and remember her at breakfast when I can no longer taste her preserves.

Maria

Sample 8-4-1-2: Expressing condolences on the death of a business partner

Dear Mrs. Smith,

I don't know what it's like to lose someone under the circumstances that you have. But whenever someone you love is gone, there is always an empty spot in our life. I can imagine that you're hurting just like all of us who knew Robert. Those of us who knew Robert could tell that he loved you very much. I hope you are surrounded with your own friends and family that can comfort you during this terrible time.

Sample 8-4-1-3: Expressing condolences on the death of a business partner

Dear Sirs,

We were distressed to read in International Daily this morning that your president had died and I am writing at once to express our deep sympathy.

I had the privilege of knowing Mr. Smith for many years and always regarded him as a personal friend. By his untimely passing our industry has lost one of its ablest leaders. We, at this moment, recall his many kindnesses and it was always a pleasure to do business with him. He will be greatly missed by all who know him and had dealings with him.

My staff join me in conveying our sincere sympathy to his family.

Yours very sincerely,

Wang Jun

President of ABC Co. Ltd

8.4.2 Writing a consolation

Useful phrases for expressing consolation

(1) Please accept my most sincere sympathy and best wishes.

(2) Please convey our sympathy and our warm regards to Mr. Smith, your president.

(3) I was deeply sorry to hear of your illness and write to express my sympathy and most earnest good wishes for your speedy recovery.

(4) I'm shocked to learn that a fire broke out in your office this morning.

(5) I'm stunned to learn that you were injured in the accident.

(6) I've learned you sustained a heavy loss in a burglary last night. We offer you our sincerest regrets for your misfortune.

(7) All of us at the Guangzhou Trading Company were sorry to hear about the extensive fire damage which your company has sustained.

(8) All of us at ABC Company would like to extend our deepest sympathy to you.

Sample 8-4-2-1: Consoling a patient

Dear Mary,

You are missed. It's awfully quiet around here without you.

I'm so glad your surgery went well. Now comes the hard part—taking it easy. This will be a whole new experience for you, the perpetual-motion machine. Please take your time. The body has a marvelous healing process, but it sometimes works more slowly than we'd like.

With heartfelt prayers for your recovery.

Sincerely yours,

John

Sample 8-4-2-2: Consoling a friend suffering from a flood

Dear Mr. and Mrs. White,

It was really bad luck to have the flood hit you so hard. I know how much you love that house. I'm glad that neither of you was injured and the damage wasn't any worse.

I hope that the repairs are going smoothly, and you will soon have your house and your peace of upset mind back in order again. If I can be of any help, just call me anytime.

Yours sincerely,

Mr. and Mrs. Green

Sample 8-4-2-3: Consoling a friend suffering from an earthquake

Dear Mr. Smith,

I was extremely sorry to hear of the earthquake which destroyed your beautiful house in Washington. I know well how much that house meant to you and Mrs. Smith, and I hasten to offer my deepest sympathy.

Nevertheless, I was most relieved to learn that none of your family members suffered serious injury, although my heart still aches when I think of the great number of people who were killed or seriously injured in this unprecedented tragedy.

If there is anything I can do for you and your family, please do not hesitate to let me know.

Sincerely yours,

Wang Jun

Sample 8-4-2-4: Consoling a friend injured in a car accident

Dear Mr. Yang,

I was very sorry to hear when I called at your office today, that you had been injured in a car accident, but equally relieved to learn that you are now making satisfactory progress in the Center Hospital.

In a long talk with Miss Lin, your secretary, I was told business is quite good and your company has received many orders for your newly-designed shirt.

With modern facilities in the Center Hospital, you will be all right and back in your office again very soon.

I am sending you some flowers and a little fruit, with my sincere wishes for your quick recovery.

Yours faithfully,

Tom White

Ex. 8-4-1

Directions: *One of your former schoolmates has passed away from illness. Write to comfort his/her parents.*

8.5 Letter of Congratulations

8.5.1 Dos and don'ts for writing effective letters of congratulations

(1) Write the congratulation letter as soon as possible after the fortunate event takes place.

(2) State in the beginning the specific occasion that has motivated you to write a congratulation letter.

(3) Express praise and approval of the reader's accomplishment in your congratulation letter.

(4) Keep your congratulation letter simple and concise (under one page in length).

(5) Don't suggest that the fortunate event should benefit the letter-writer in any way.

(6) Don't exaggerate your congratulatory words, or your letter may seem sarcastic or mocking.

(7) Keep your letter positive and don't include any negative comments or unhappy news.

8.5.2 Useful phrases for letters of congratulations

(1) I'm very pleased to hear of your recent promotion to the manager of Technology Department.

(2) It is with the greatest pleasure that I offer you my sincere congratulations on your success.

(3) Please accept my warmest congratulations on this 20th anniversary of the founding of your business.

(4) I am delighted to hear of your appointment as Chairman of the Board and wish to offer my very sincere congratulations.

(5) Congratulations to you and every good wish for your success and happiness in your new position!

(6) Sincere congratulations from the bottom of my heart on your marriage.

(7) I must write this line to congratulate you most heartily on your happy marriage. I wish you the best of everything for all the years ahead.

(8) Allow me to congratulate you on your National Day.

(9) Congratulations on your graduation and hope the future will bring you success and a whole wide world of happiness.

(10) I am pleased to hear of little Mary's birth. Congratulations to all the three of you!

(11) I wish you plenty of prosperity and good luck in your new house.

(12) May happiness and good health accompany you and your family in your new house.

Sample 8-5-2-1: Congratulations on birthday

Dear Rose,

I recall that your birthday is just around the corner and suppose your family is planning some surprise for you. Being far apart on both sides of the ocean, I cannot stretch my hand to shake with you. So I send the E-mail to offer you my heartiest congratulations and best wishes for many happy returns of your birthday.

Yours affectionately,

Sample 8-5-2-2: Wedding congratulations

Dear Paul,

Your wedding card brings to me the happy news of your marriage. I congratulate you and trust that your marriage will be a source of blessing and happiness to you both.

Please accept this little present with my congratulations upon your happy wedding.

Yours very sincerely,

Sample 8-5-2-3: Congratulations on starting a business

Dear Jack Green,

How wonderful it is to learn your new branch will be open and be ready for business—congratulations!

With your experience and proved capability in the trade, I know your organization will be a huge success.

Please accept my warmest congratulations and best wishes.

Sincerely,

Sample 8-5-2-4: Season's greetings

Dear Mr. Green,

On the occasion of New Year, may my wife and I extend to you and your wife our sincere greetings.

Wish you a happy New Year, your career greater success and your family happiness.

Sincerely,

Sample 8-5-2-5: Season's greetings

Dear Mr. Smith,

As 2014 draws to a close, may I take a moment to say thank you so much for the support you have given us throughout the year.

May all the joys and blessings of Christmas be yours, and may the coming year bring you prosperity and happiness!

With my best personal regards,

> **Note:**
> In the practice of personal letters, it is likely to include some skills of other types of writing, such as the skills of writing descriptive or narrative paragraphs, for instance, when you need to talk about yourself and introduce something new to the receivers, like a letter of complaint or a letter of request.

Ex. 8-5-1

Directions: Suppose you are the Chairman of ABC Company. On the occasion of the tenth business anniversary of CBA Company, send congratulations to Mr. Liu Ming, president of CBA Company, your business partner.

Chapter Nine

Applying for University Admission

Introduction

Application procedures for admission to a program of study abroad depend on the type of institution, the level of the course and the subject of study. There is much flexibility, but a typical diary of events may be like this:

(1) Contact the university to obtain an application form and prospectus, or download the application form from the Internet.

(2) Read the prospectus carefully to get guidance on how to complete the form.

(3) Fill in the application form and post it to the university's admission office. You may have to submit a Personal Statement as well, or a Synopsis of proposed research project, if the university requires so.

(4) (If accepted) Receive from the university the letter of acceptance (or Admission Notice), with which you may apply for your passport and visa.

9.1 Requesting for an Admission Form

Sample 9-1-1

Dear Sir:

I wish to pursue a doctoral degree in Chemistry Engineering at your university. My desired date of entrance is fall, 2013. Please send me necessary application forms at your early convenience.

If possible, I also wish to obtain a graduate assistantship so that I can support myself and obtain more experience while pursing graduating study.

I obtained my B. E (Chemical Engineering) and M. E (Environmental Protection) from Tsinghua University. At present, I work as a teacher at the same university.

I have taken TOEFL and received a score of 113. I am going to take GRE general test this coming

October.

Would you please send me the application forms for admission and financial support? Thank you very much.

Sincerely yours,
Zhang Qiang

Sample 9-1-2

Dear Professor Smith,

  I am writing to you about the possibility of further studies in the field of Computer Engineering leading to the Ph. D. degree at your institution. I would also like to apply for a position as a teaching or research assistant, or any other financial aids available for foreign students. Would you please send me the necessary information and forms?

  I am 25, male, majoring in computer science. I received my B. E (Computer Science) in June, 1993 and M. E (Computer Science) in March, 1996 from Tsinghua University in Beijing. I kept on ranking top in my undergraduate class (50 students) and graduate class (30 students). I do believe that the doctorate-oriented study at your institution is of great help for my further study in the area of Computer Science.

  I have taken the TOEFL Test (score 114) and GRE General Test (score 2,170).

  Thank you very much. I am looking forward to hearing from you soon.

Sincerely yours,

Sample 9-1-3

Dear Sir,

  I am a graduate of Beijing Foreign Studies University majoring in English with a B. A. degree from English Department. After graduation, I concentrated on studying English linguistics and obtained my M. A. degree from this University in 1995. With a view to getting some advanced studies, I am writing to you to apply for admission to your university to pursue a Doctor's degree in English Linguistics. I'm also applying for a scholarship which will enable me to come to your university sooner.

  Hoping to be favored with an early reply.

Sincerely yours,
Liu Dong

Sample 9-1-4

P. O Box 9705

International Trade Department

Xiamen University

Xiamen, 361005
P. R. China
10 February 2001

Postgraduate Office
Leeds University Business School
11 Blenheim Terrance
Leeds
England LS2 9JT

Dear Sirs,

    I am a student in the International Trade Department of Xiamen University, China, expecting to graduate with a Bachelor's degree this summer. I learned of your graduate programme two years ago at the "British Education Exhibition 2010," held in Xiamen in October 2010. I am writing to seek enrollment for the 2013 academic year. If possible, I would also like to apply for a position of Graduate Assistantship.

    I should be obliged if you could send me the application form and prospectus.

    I should be pleased to forward my credentials, such as references, transcripts, and photocopies of IELTS scores.

    I look forward to hearing from you.

Yours faithfully,
Dong Ling

Ex. 9-1

Directions: *Use your college library or search from the Internet and write a letter of application to a university (in Britain or in the USA), applying for admission into your chosen programme (MA, Msc, etc).*

9.2 Graduation Certification and Notarization

A certificate is an official document affirming some fact.

Sample 9-2-1

Graduation Certification

    This is to certificate that Li Xiaoxue, female, native of Shijiazhuang, Hebei, China, was born in November, 1980. She was enrolled to study English in Department of Foreign Languages and Literature, Beijing Normal University, 1998, and graduated in July, 2002.

The following is the report of the academic records in her specialized course from the first to the eighth semesters.

1st Semester:

1. Basic English (Oral exam): Good; (Written exam): Excellent.

2. Phonetics (Exam): Good.

3. Grammar (Test): Pass.

...

7th semester:

1. English Reading (Exam): Excellent.

2. Listening (Test): Pass.

3. Monographic Grammar (Test): Pass.

8th Semester:

1. English Reading (Exam): Excellent.

2. English Composition (Exam): Excellent.

Notarization:

The act of notarization is to certify or attest to (the validity of a signature on a document, for example) as a notary public.

Sample 9-2-2

NOTARIZATION

This is to notarize that Cheng Fen (male, born in 1971) was enrolled in the Foreign Languages Department of Shandong University (a 4-year course) in September, 1988 and graduated in July, 1992.

Jinan Notary Public Office

(Seal)

Notary: Zhang Li

(Signature)

July 19, 1993

9.3 Personal Statement

9.3.1 Contents of a personal statement

Many universities require applicants to submit personal statements when the applicants make applications. Your personal statement is your opportunity to persuade the admission officers to offer you a place (or an award) in preference to your competitors.

Things to be included in a personal statement are:

(1) Your reasons for choosing the course/award.

(2) The background to your interest in the subject (academic qualifications and professional training).

(3) The work experiences (employment, work shadowing, voluntary work, etc.) and/or personal developments which have been most important to you and which are relevant to your application.

(4) Research (experience, skills, scope of study, achievements, etc.) to demonstrate your potentials.

(5) Future career plans.

Apart from the above, you may also detail other interests and activities, or emphasize your character (attributes such as dedication, thoughtfulness, compassion, maturity, leadership, etc.).

9.3.2 Essential qualities of a good personal statement

Admission officers look for motivation and character. They want to know whether you have good academic reasons for wanting to study in their institution and whether you have had enough training/qualifications to ensure the success of your further academic pursuit.

The secret of a good personal statement is, probably, a natural and unpretentious style. There is no need to resort to flourishing language, or to try to flatter the university by telling them how prestigious they are, or how beautiful their campus is. They know this already. What they want to know is more about you. In saying things about yourself, avoid emotive and adjectives like "excellent," "remarkable," "great," "wonderful," etc. Such high-sounding and vague modifiers would only produce a negative effect—being insincere or self-conceited.

Sample 9-3-1

Personal Statement

Born and bought up in a remote township in Southwest China, I witnessed the hardship and the straitened life of the people in the mountain areas, where many children of my age were denied the chance of schooling. Therefore, I should cherish the precious opportunity at university and must study against time. What I kept in my mind was the only idea of studying—studying for the folks in my hometown, for the Chinese people, studying to bring a new appearance to my poor hometown. Thus stimulated, I always feel an insatiable curiosity for the new and an inexhaustible drive to push forward. In a sense, it is the arduous social conditions in my hometown that have cultivated my simple, honest personality and shaped my industrious and enterprising spirit.

Looking back to the past years, I am very grateful to my dear teachers. Under their tireless instructions and guidance, I have made steady progress in my academic pursuit—not only have I laid a solid foundation in chemistry theory, experimental know-how, but also I have built up my academic ego: rigorous scientific attitude and original creativity of my own.

I usually work hard at my lessons. For example, I like to get up early—usually one hour earlier than my roommates—and spend the precious morning hour reading and listening to the English broadcast. I am the first undergraduate of my grade to have taken TOEFL test, with a score above 100. I like to study ahead of the teacher's schedule and never feel satisfied with in-class explanation of textbooks alone. I usually spend hours reading reference books after class, so as to enrich my knowledge reservoir. The library is one of my favorite places to stay in, and frequenting bookstores is my hobby in my spare time.

As my teachers have commented, I am good at independent thinking and like to probe into things by asking "why." For example, I like to approach the same question from different angles and air my views that might sound different from others, for I believe this is the right way to gain quicker progress academically. This characteristic of mine is highly appraised by my teachers and fellow students. Consequently, I have kept an excellent school record ever since the first school year, ranking at the top of my grade. I have been awarded Outstanding-student Scholarship of Sichuan University for three years running.

Two years ago, my father, a local government official who was then making an on-spot-investigation in U.S.A., paid a special visit to Stanford University, where he was deeply impressed by the most sophisticated education facilities and development in science and technology. As I learnt from him later, there are so many marvelous things about U.S.A. which revealed the present state of universities in USA: the first-class scientific and technical equipment and educational means, the latest and exciting breakthroughs and developments in scientific researches, galaxies of scholars of world fame, lively academic atmosphere at university… And since then, I have made up my mind to pursue my postgraduate education in USA, right upon my graduation.

I wish to continue my studies on chemistry or relevant specialties. If my request is granted, I would endeavor to make the best use of this golden opportunity, trying my best to make greater progress academically. I hope by the time when I have had my Ph. D., I will be able to stay there for another year or so, engaging in some post-doctorate program. And then, armed with the most advanced knowledge and experience acquired from USA, I will return to my motherland to work as a chemistry professor at my Alma Mater. In this case, the dream of my childhood will have become true and I will be able to make greater contributions to Chinese chemistry science and serve my people and peoples all over the world wholeheartedly.

Sample 9-3-2

Personal Statement

As a 21-year-old aspiring student majoring in Journalism in Shandong University, who has grown up in pace with the evolution of China's opening and reform over the previous several decades, I am keenly aware of the overwhelming change of the life and the society in China. What I am eager to do is to learn and master the knowledge and expertise to not only observe but also record what I see in my life.

My interest in journalism dates back to my years in high school years when I worked as the Chinese class representative throughout the six years. Due to the influence of my parents, who are both editors working for People's Daily, I have been passionate about reading newspapers and writing articles related to local and national affairs. My first step in the direction of journalism began with the opening of our high school radio station in 1999, in which I was in charge of collecting news materials and writing news releases. My devotion to the radio station persevered throughout the whole high school years, regardless of the pressure from the National College Entrance Examination.

My passion for journalism continued after I was enrolled in the Department of Journalism, Shandong University, where I was exposed to a wide range of knowledge and people in the profession and greatly equipped myself with the systematic professional knowledge and skills in journalism, design, printing, publishing, editing and photography. As a top student in my class, I was lucky enough to be recruited in my second term into "Outlook International," an influential nationwide news website in China, to work as a spare time news reporter covering the events in Ji'nan city, the capital city of Shandong province. Throughout the two-year working experience in Outlook International, I have developed interview and communication techniques, organizing, writing and editing skills and being able to see and analyze facts and data from different perspectives.

Besides my major journalism, I also chose to study English and Japanese as two minors and read widely in the two languages, including classics and modern essays, because I believe multiple-language proficiency would be an invaluable advantage to have when working in the area of communication.

In addition to my study and work, extracurricular interests such as reading and music enriched my college life. Music, in particular, is a great love of mine. I regularly attend concerts and have been an active member of the "Campus Green" for over two years, which entails promoting publicity through flyers and posters for the college band. Another one of my interests is the Internet. I contribute articles to the college website dealing with important student matters. My article covering college canteen renovation was the most viewed essay on the website in the year.

Upon completing my undergraduate program, I am thinking of pursuing a master's degree before becoming a professional journalist in the future. With the necessary academic and professional foundation from college, I believe an overseas education can help me broaden my outlook, enrich my knowledge and skills and lay a foundation for my future.

Yours sincerely,

Comments: In the two Personal Statements, both authors express very clearly what they want to do and how well they are prepared to pursue their ambitions. They explain their interests and incorporate different past experiences, hence, giving a perfect picture of what they have done and their relevance to what they want to do in the future.

9.4 Letter of Recommendation

An applicant should have his/her letters of recommendation submitted from professors or others who can assess the quality of his/her academic performance, capability and potential of research.

Nearly every graduate program requires applicants to submit letters of recommendation. Don't underestimate the importance of these letters. While your transcript, standardized test scores and personal statement are vital components to your graduate school application, an excellent letter of recommendation can make up for weaknesses in any of these areas.

A well written letter of recommendation provides admission committees with information that isn't found elsewhere in the application. A letter of recommendation is a detailed discussion, from a faculty member, of the personal qualities, accomplishments and experiences that make you unique and perfect for the programs to which you've applied.

Admission to any institute of higher learning usually requires one or more letters of recommendation. Graduate programs often require the submission of two or more letters and frequently follow specifically outlined procedures for their creation and submission. Be sure to follow these instructions closely.

Letters of recommendation required for admission to post-graduate studies are typically written by a faculty member, an academic advisor or an administrator. In some cases, an employer can write the letter if academic recommendations are not available. These letters provide the admissions committee with information not found in the application—information that shows the applicant matches the school's expectations and requirements. The letter also provides an opportunity for an applicant to be seen as an individual and helps him/her to stand out from the hundreds or thousands of other applicants.

It is important that the person providing the recommendation has a good understanding of your academic history, interests, goals and direction. Normally, this type of recommendation letter is addressed to a specific person and should be submitted along with the admission application or as outlined in the admissions procedure. In many cases, accredited universities require that letters of recommendation be sent directly to specific departments or to the admissions office. If this is the case, the applicant may be required to sign a waiver of confidentiality and relinquish his/her right to access the information contained in the letter or forms. Academic letters of recommendation may contain evidence or confirmation of the following:

(1) Academic performance.
(2) Honors and awards.
(3) Initiative, dedication, integrity, reliability, etc.
(4) Willingness to follow school policy.
(5) Ability to work with others.
(6) Ability to work independently.

Choose who will represent you wisely. No one person can represent you accurately in all areas. Find someone who knows your strengths in the areas where you need to satisfy the requirements of a particular employer or admission board. Schedule a convenient time for you and your employer or advisor to meet. Review the requirements and expectations of the recommendation letter. This process helps the person who is writing the letter answer questions, clarify points that may need elaboration and point out additional information that may be required. Make this process easy by providing all of the information needed so that you can obtain an accurate and positive recommendation.

When you request a recommendation, communicate your needs in a straightforward way. Explain what you are applying for and ask if the person can provide you with a good recommendation. If someone exhibits any uneasiness about providing you with a strong recommendation, be polite, thank him/her for their time and then look elsewhere. Choose someone who:

(1) Can provide a well-written letter.

(2) Knows you well enough to be credible.

(3) Thinks highly of you and your abilities.

(4) Holds a respected position.

Keep in mind that the recommender is doing you a favor and has a busy schedule with other commitments. Make sure you allow enough time so that he/she can provide you with a well-written and effective letter.

Tips: Writing your own letter of recommendation

Do not be surprised if a person you are asking for a recommendation asks you to write a first draft of the letter that he/she will then modify and sign. Begin by providing an accurate assessment of your strengths without dwelling on limitations. Letters of recommendation are intended to be positive and realistic evaluations of performance, competence and capability. Do not be shy in communicating your strengths. Look at the following suggestions.

(1) List your strengths, talents and abilities. These may include diligence, punctuality, leadership, reliability, enthusiasm, creativity, independence, teamwork, organization, etc.

(2) Highlight your strengths and accomplishments without bragging.

(3) Choose several of your qualities and strengths that match the current situation and do not list everything you have ever done.

(4) Use a professional vocabulary and style and write as if you were the employer providing the letter.

Sample 9-4-1

A Letter of Recommendation

Dear Sir,

I am writing this letter to recommend Mr. Zhang Qiang, one of my former students, for his advanced studies at your university.

A gifted student of all-round development, Mr. Zhang possesses such good qualities as diligence, team spirit, friendliness and the readiness to help others. Rarely have I found such a student of good character and fine scholarship during dozens of years of my teaching career. What is more, as a bright student, he not only has a solid elementary knowledge, wide scope of learning, but also good qualities of insatiable curiosity and independent thinking, which enabled him to top his classmates in almost every course ever since the first school year. Consequently, he has been awarded Excellent-student Scholarship of the university for three years in succession.

An honest, upright, enthusiastic and cheerful boy, Mr. Zhang is a good organizer and an active participator of all kinds of academic and social activities. His strong personality, which is manifested in his exceptional organizational ability, intense sympathy for others and selfless devotion to his task, has made a deep impression on all people he gets along with.

Therefore, it is with great pleasure that I recommend Mr. Zhang for studying as a graduate student in the Chemistry Department of your university. I am convinced that he will prove to be a promising student with still greater academic achievements in the near future and a valuable acquisition to your university.

Sincerely yours
Li Guodong
Professor of Chemistry Department

Chapter Ten
Employment Writing

Introduction

When applying for a job, you may need a Cover Letter (CL), a Résumé or a Curriculum Vitae (CV). A cover letter usually goes with a résumé or a CV. They bear similar features: clear and concise content and customized for each position applied for. This chapter is dedicated to the three types of writing for employment: cover letter, résumé and CV.

10.1 Cover Letter

When applying for a job, a cover letter should be sent or posted with your résumé or CV. Your cover letter should be specific to the position you are applying for, relating your skills and experience to those noted in the job posting. Your cover letter is your first (and best) chance to make a good impression.

An effective cover letter should explain the reasons for your interest in the organization and in the job you are applying for. Take the time to review sample cover letters, and then make sure that your letter explains how your skills relate to the criteria listed in the job posting.

Make sure to put yourself in the employer's shoes, i.e., write it to the point and make it well-structured and easy to read within 30 seconds or less.

Parts of a cover letter

1. Introduction

In the introduction, you should provide the following information:

(1) Why writing this cover letter (job posting, career fair, networking contact, area of interest).

(2) Why wanting to work for the company/what interests you about the position.

(3) Demonstrating your knowledge of the organization.

2. Body

Sell the skills and abilities you have as required for the position (briefly). Back the skills up with specific examples, state why you would be a good fit.

3. Close

Thank them, request an interview or meeting and indicate how to contact you.

> **Note:**
> If seeking job opportunities in the Hidden Job Market, indicate how and when you will contact the employer in order to follow up.

Tips:

- Always send a CL with your résumé if unable to hand it over;
- Should be addressed to a specific person. **NEVER** use "To whom it may concern…";
- Should be typed on the same paper as your résumé;
- Should be attractive, well laid out and kept to **ONE** page;
- Write a different cover letter for each job you apply for. **NOT** a form cover letter;
- Construct it by using the company information.

> **Note:**
> When sending your cover letter via e-mail, always send the text letter in the body of the e-mail message unless an attachment is required, as some employers do not open attachment because of the virus risk.

Sampe 10-1-1: A cover letter

Peggy S. Smith
762 Ridge Road
Lafayette, IN 47905
peggysmith843@e-mail-link.com
765-555-8493
June 21, 2001

Nancy Thompson, Human Resources Manager
Galvan Group
374 Tomsdale Ave.
Chicago, IL 60614

Dear Ms. Thompson:

As an experienced professional in the building service contracting industry, I am applying for the position of Customer Service Manager, advertised on your website (galvangroup12.com). A successful background in the areas of customer service and operations would make me a valuable asset to your company.

Providing quality customer service is a major focus of my present position with MKC Associates. Galvan Group is known as a top-notch company in many areas, especially customer service. I would like to put my customer service experience to work for you. As we both know, it is a competitive market today and superior customer service is what makes the difference. Managing a customer base of 75 facilities throughout Indiana for the past seven years has sharpened my customer service skills tremendously.

In the last seven years, our employee turnover rate has gone from 150% to 55%. Part of that can be attributed to the development and recognition programs I have instituted, including Christmas parties and summer picnics. Employees need to feel they are part of a "team" and at Galvan Group, that would be one of my goals.

Six years ago, I set a personal goal to continue my education at Purdue University. In December of this year, that goal will be achieved and I will receive a Bachelor of Science in Organizational Leadership and Supervision. I am proud of this accomplishment, as I have worked full-time while attending Purdue part-time; my GPA is 3.6/4.0. In addition, my skills with Galvan Group would be a great opportunity for me to take on a new challenge while fulfilling my commitment to customer service.

I am anxious to talk with you and discuss my potential to contribute to your organization. I will contact you in three days to discuss my application. You can reach me at 765-555-8493, or by e-mail at peggysmith843@e-mail-link.com. Thank you for your time and consideration.

Sincerely,
Peggy S. Smith (signature)
(Peggy S. Smith)

10.2 Résumé

10.2.1 The purpose of people writing a résumé

People write résumé when they want to communicate their experience, skills and education related to a specific position to an employer, and use it as a job search tool providing them with their first opportunity to "market themselves" to an employer.

10.2.2 Types of résumés

There are three types of résumés commonly accepted.

1. Chronological résumé

It is a traditional format commonly used when one's experience is presented in reverse date order.

2. Functional résumé

It focuses on your skills and experience rather than on your chronological work history. It is typically used by job seekers who are changing careers or who have gaps in their employment history. It can be very effective for recent graduates with limited experience.

3. Transferable skills résumé

It combines the features of both Chronological Résumés and Functional Résumés, and highlights your key skills/special strengths.

10.2.3 General tips for the scannable résumé

- Focus on nouns, not action verbs;
- Don't fold or staple;
- Should be laser printed on white paper;
- Use popular sans serif font (example: Helvetica, Arial);
- Maximize the use of industry jargon;
- Each phone number should be on the same line;
- To and from dates should be on the same line;
- Utilize a keywords section to maximize hits;
- Use asterisks, plus signs or hyphens to make it more visually appealing.

10.2.4 Other sections (may be included) in a résumé

S1. Research philosophy (overview, major contributions, career, effort, etc.);

S2. Major publications (first…);

S3. Conference and symposia;

S4. External professional activities;

S5. Future plans.

Sample 10-2-1

A Résumé:

Mary J. Morris
"The Larches"
Spottonham Road

Larswick
Lincs
SP12 5MS
Tel: 01854 658194

Experience

1994—present
- *Education and Publications Officer, Boston Museum.*
- *Responsible for organizing annual program of school visits, lectures, and holiday courses.*
- *In charge of liaison with primary and secondary schools.*
- *Preparing and publishing a range of leaflets and "mini-guides" to the Museum's collection. Managing an annual budget of £10,000.*

1989—1994
- *Head of Humanities, Larswick Middle School.*
- *Teaching history, geography and religious education.*
- *Preparing and administering departmental policy documents.*
- *Member of School's Senior Management team.*
- *Pastoral care tutor to 35 pupils.*
- *Responsible for the school magazine.*

1985—1989
- *Teacher of History at St Wulfstan's High School, Scunthorpe.*
- *Teaching pupils across full ability and age range (11-18).*
- *Preparing classes for GCE "O" level and GCSE examinations, and GCE "A" levels and university entrance.*
- *House tutor.*

Education/qualifications and training
- *Postgraduate Certificate in Education, University of Hull.*
- *BA Honours 2nd class, History and Economics, York University.*
- *"A" level English, History, French.*
- *"O" level English language, English literature, Maths, French, History, Geography, Biology.*

Interests
- *Mountain walking.*

- Foreign travel.
- Voluntary social work with local women's refuge.

Referees

Dr P. J. Cleary, Mrs S. P. Greenwick,

Director, 34 High Street,

Boston Museum, Brentham,

Boston, Surrey,

Lincs, GU23 9BV

BO1 2RF

Sample 10-2-2

A Résumé

Charles Morris

Current residency: Taipei, Taiwan of China

Nationality: Canadian

Tel: 0911-622-345

Email: ***charles.morris@gmail.com***

HIGHLIGHTS OF ABILITIES

- Creating training programs based on employee needs
- Coaching and encouraging employees to develop themselves further
- Helping companies form cross-functional teams

EDUCATION

- Master of Business Administration, University of Toronto, Toronto, Canada
- Bachelor of Arts, major in Political Science, University of Guelf, Ontario, Canada

WORK EXPERIENCE

Jan 2012—Current

- Senior Consultant—McKin Consulting Company
- Concentrating on HR training and consulting for multinational companies in Taiwan of China

Jan 2008—2011

- Consultant—A.B.C. Communications
- Consulting with high-level managers, specializing in presentation and negotiation skills

May 2005— 2007

- *Business Instructor—DE Company*
- *Taught presentation skills and writing*

HOBBIES
- *Traveling, Reading, Skiing*

REFERENCES
Abdul Rahman, Andrew William
McKin Consulting Company
0911-677-326

> **Note:**
> There is no one right way to create a résumé. Your résumé will be and should be as individual as you are.

Tips:
When sending your résumé via e-mail:
- Unless an attachment is required, always send the text résumé version in the body of the e-mail message as some employers do not open attachment b/c for fear of the danger of virus.
- Always include a cover letter (unless told otherwise) in the body of the message before the résumé.
- Send only one e-mail with both the cover letter and résumé included. And use the job title or reference number in the subject line of the message.

10.3 Curriculum Vitae

10.3.1 When to use a CV?

A curriculum vitae is used primarily when you apply for academic education and a scientific or research position. It is also applicable when you apply for a fellowship or grant.

10.3.2 What's the difference between CV and résumé?

A curriculum vitae is a longer (up to two or more pages) and more detailed synopsis of your background and skills. A CV includes a summary of your educational and academic backgrounds as well as teaching and research experience, publications, presentations, awards, honors, affiliations and other details.

10.3.3　Tips on writing a successful CV

- There are some common sections you should cover: personal and contact information; education and qualifications; work history and/or experience; relevant skills to the job in question; interests, achievements or hobbies; and some references.

- A successful CV is always carefully and clearly presented. The layout should always be clean and well structured. In addition, CVs should never be crumpled or folded, so you should use an A4 envelope to post your applications.

- Always remember the CV hotspot—the upper middle area of the first page—is where the recruiter's eyes will naturally fall, so make sure you include your most important information there.

- Stick to no more than two pages of A4.
- Tailor the CV to the position you are applying for.
- Make the most of your skills, interests and experiences.
- Make sure you include dates on all the publications you include.

Sample 10-3-1

CURRICULUM VITAE

Janice Moore

Department of English
Boston University
881 Commonwealth Avenue
Boston, MA 02215
USA

Nationality: the United States
Resident of : Boston, US
Professional Title: Associate Professor
E-mail: **william.moore@hotmail.com**
Mobile: 1-617-703-2008

UNIVERSITY DEGREES

　　1998—PhD English, Yale University
　　1994—MA, English, Yale University
　　1992—BA, English, Yale University

CAREER

　　2009—current　　Associate Professor, Department of English, Boston University
　　2005—2009　　Associate Professor, Department of English, University of Florida
　　2001—2005　　Assistant Professor, Department of English, University of Clark
　　1999—2001　　Postdoctoral fellow, Department of English, Boston University

1998—1999   Lecturer, Department of English, Yale University

PUBLICATIONS
BOOKS

1. *The Woman's Page: Journalism and Rhetoric.* New York: University of New York Press, 2014
2. *Animals in Modern Literary Imagination.* New York: University of New York Press, 2012
3. *Sick Spirit:On the Work of Mary Lee.* New York: University of New York Press, 2008
4. *Truths of Storytelling.* New York: University of New York Press, 2004

PAPERS

1. "The Storytelling of Mansfield." *Academic Questions* 26 (2013): 329-332
2. "Encounters with Self: The Role of the Sublime in Anna Moodie's Writing. *Etudes Canadiennes/Canadian Studies* 53 (Dec, 2012): 101-116
3. "The Lost Identity of Amily." *Connotations: A Journal for Critical Debate* 19,1-3 (2010):34-51
4. "The Door of No Return: the Work of Thomas William." *American Literature* 182 (Autumn, 2009): 13-28
5. "Bring Back Learning." *Academic Questions* 25 (2008):124-134
6. "No Way Out." *Critics* 12(2005):67-73

AWARDS

Google Research Award in Boston University, 2012
Young Research Scholar Award in University of Florida, 2008

COURSES TAUGHT

Introduction to American Literature
A Century of American Women Writers
Nineteenth-Century American Literature
Regionalism in Twentieth-Century American Fiction
Canadian Literature
Literary Theories

ACADEMIC INTERESTS

Women's Writing, Modern American Literature, Canadian Literature, Theory

CURRENT RESEARCH

I'm currently devoted to the study of the characteristics of modern women's writing. With the project "Modern American Women Writers' Storytelling" I'm involved in, I'd like to detect the relationship between the way of telling stories and the identity of women writers.

REFERENCES

Thomas Hammer, Jame Brown
University of Boston
617-723-7865

Ex. 10-1

Directions: *Write a cover letter. Include the following information:*

- *You have just graduated from BIT and are looking for a job;*
- *You read an employment ad. on a vacancy in Beijing Evening Daily;*
- *Enclose your résumé or CV.*

Chapter Eleven
Note and Memo

Introduction

A notes is something that you write down to remind you of something and also a short information letter. It is a short message of everyday practice. For example, in an office, there are delivery notes (documents showing that goods have been delivered), diplomatic notes (formal letters from one government to another) and promissory notes (documents promising to pay money before particular dates). For individuals, there are some notes of other functions, such as a thank-you note, a quick note or a sick note, all of which are commonly applied both in office service and in everyday life. For example, when you want to memorize some events or important dates, when you want to warn both yourself and others of something and when you have to say something with some other people you have already engaged before but unfortunately you are away on some other business, you need to leave a note or a memo to convey your ideas and thoughts on your desk, stick it on your door, or on your computer, etc. Quite often, it is also found on the door of an office or a house, on the gate/entrance and on a bulletin board. Memos are short official notes to another person, especially in the same company or organization. Both notes and memos serve well in transferring information.

Although sometimes you can find that there are some formatted ready-to-use note pads selling in some stationeries and bookstores, it is easy to design on your own for special or individual purposes, which you will feel quite useful.

The same as Cover Letters and CVs, there are no mechanical ways of creating notes and memos. When designing your own notes and memos, remember the following advice. There are some omissions such as addresses of the addressee and the addresser, the beginning "Dear" and the ending "Sincerely" and the "year" within the date/time.

> **Tips:**
> - Memos should generally be direct and concise, almost telegraphic;
> - Remember the format of a memo.
>
> You may create your own memo pads and have them printed in most cases.

Sample 11-1: Leaving a message

```
Date: _____
To: _____
From: _____
Subject: _____
_____
_____
_____
              or: (Date)
```

(While you were out)

```
For: _____
Date: _____
Time: _____

Message: _____
_____
_____
_____
```

Sample 11-2: Double-function memo

Date:	‡	While you were out _____
To:_____	‡	(For)_____
From:_____	‡	(Date)_____
Subject:_____	‡	(Time)_____
_____	‡	
_____	‡	(Message)_____
or: (Date)	‡	_____

Sample 11-3: User-friendly memo

```
For_____
Date_____
Time_____

WHILE YOU WERE OUT
_____

From_____

Phone No._____
  ☐ TELEPHONED      ☐ URGENT
  ☐ PLEASE CALL     ☐ WANT TO SEE YOU
  ☐ WILL CALL AGAIN ☐ CAME TO SEE YOU
  ☐ RETURNED YOUR CALL
  ☐ CHECK YOUR EMAIL
Other Message_____
_____
```

Sample 11-4: A request, or an engagement on a sheet of paper or pad

April 11

Hellen,

Could we see each other for about an hour on Friday afternoon at 3 o'clock?

Marry

Sample 11-5: A short message for apology

Tues. Oct. 20

Dear Prof. ×××

I am sorry I couldn't make our 4 o'clock appointment. Prof. ×'s lecture lasted a lot longer than I expected. I could meet you in the Dept. office tomorrow at 3 pm, if that is convenient for you. If not, please leave a note in my mailbox, #529, before tomorrow morning.

Thank you.

Jerry

Sample 11-6: An informal invitation

Mr. Johnson,

  There will be a ball held for my sister's 18th birthday on next Sunday evening, July 7, at 6 in my apartment. We should like to invite you to attend it and we could have a talk during the breaks. Snacks and beverage are prepared. Hope you will come.

Dick

Ex. 11-1

  1. *Write a piece of memo within about 100 words to make an appointment with a girl/boy student whom you are not quite familiar with.*

  2. *Make an informal apology to your friend for your failure to fulfill your earlier appointment and give your reasons in sincere words.*

Chapter Twelve
Notice and Poster

Introduction

Notices are written or printed statements that give information or warning to people. For example, the notice on the wall saying "No Smoking," a notice about a meeting or an obituary notice in a newspaper about people who have just died. Notices should be brief, easy to understand, polite and relevant.

Posters are large printed notices, pictures or photographs used to advertise something or as a decoration, such as a movie poster, a concert poster, a poster for an election, etc.

There are some details, for instance, some information about the lecturer, the meeting, the place to visit, the keynote speaker or the research field announced when needed.

Tips on the layout of a notice:
- Use a different size font to emphasize the heading.
- Leave space between the heading and different sections.
- Use capitals, bold letters and italics to distinguish information.
- Use sub-headings to break up the main information logically.

Sample 12-1: A notice for a lecture

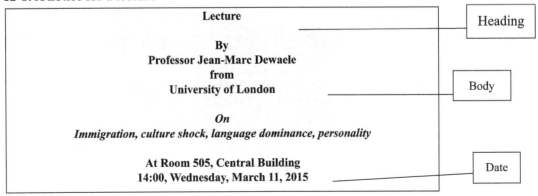

Sample 12-2: A notice for a get-together

> Department of Sociology
> End of Term Celebration
>
> Thursday, December 5, 2002
> 12:00 Noon
>
> 335 Isbister Building
>
> ALL ARE WELCOME
> TEACHING STAFF
> SENIOR SCHOLARS
> HONOUR STUDENTS
> SUPPORT STAFF
> VISITING SCHOLARS
>
> We would especially welcome some "potluck" home cooking to support this event. A sign-up sheet is available on the door of room 320.

Sample 12-3: Poster for a conference

> **Tips on writing such short messages:**
> - Right sequence of time: date(th) + month, year, e.g. 8th Aug, 2008 (read as *the eighth of August, 2008*); or: month + date, year, e.g. Oct 1, 2008 (read as: October first, 2008).
> - Abbreviation for months except May, June and July in full spelling is always welcome.
> - Short and plain words other than long or academic ones.
> e.g. abrogate→ cancel; attend→ to go; commence → start; locate → find…
> - Do not use long or elaborate, complicated phrases.
> e.g. despite the fact that→although; last but not least→last; make a purchase→buy
> - Use incomplete sentences when situation permits.
> e.g. (I'm) leaving for London immediately; (I'll be) back on Monday.
> - The addressee's and addresser's names must not be omitted; A date may be included; "dear" and "sincerely" may not be the "have to."

Ex. 12-1

1. *You will graduate from a university this summer and have many textbooks and reference books to sell. Write a notice of sales.*

2. *Suppose you are required to write a notice for help on behalf of the Student Union.*

3. *Design a poster for a lecture of a visiting scholar.*

PART FOUR
ACADEMIC WRITING

Introduction

Academic writing, one of the major essay writings, is an acknowledged central part of humanities and social sciences that is learned and taught from secondary schools to graduate schools. It betters and fosters one's qualities of insight, imagination, motivation, initiative and self-discipline that are needed not only in school task accomplishment but also in building up a life skill of wide application.

Although most students have got the experience that essay writing is not always an easy task as writing an everyday story or writing journals and dairies, they are frequently required to complete essays either during the learning or at the end of a course. One of the essential problems that most university students are facing during the courses they take and will have to accomplish is writing assignments. Accordingly, the academic essay writing becomes the basis of the so-called professional writing. However, there are certain procedures which can help learners out of the difficulties and stimulate their learning experiences.

Academic Writing in this book, in order to deal with the problem, takes you step by step through the whole process of writing a summary, a course assignment, an academic essay, a report, or a term paper from both conception and definition to completion with an effective guide to the final copy.

To reach this goal, this part is divided into three chapters: Chapter Thirteen (Summary), Chapter Fourteen (Abstract), Chapter Fifteen (Delivery).

Chapter Thirteen
Summary Writing

Introduction

To summarize an article or sometimes a whole book is to tell briefly in your own words what the article or the book is mainly about. This is an important skill in writing effectively, both in and out of itself and in communicating effectively in other kinds of writing tasks.

The general purpose of writing a summary is to present the main points or give the gist of the contents. There are several steps to follow when a summary is being written:

• Preview the work or the essay you will write the summary about, including the title, the subtitles (if any), the introduction and the conclusion.

• Look for the essay's thesis, controlling ideas and main points, and then mark them or take brief notes.

• Rearrange the main points you will use in your summary into outlines.

• Write the first draft, rewrite it and check.

13.1 Steps in Writing a Summary

When writing a summary, the writer needs to ask first: What information is essential in this material? What will show that the writer has well read it and understood it?

A good summary guides the readers to get all the main points and arguments that the author presents without the necessity of looking back to the original work.

Summary sometimes has the same features as the paraphrase. To paraphrase means to express someone else's ideas in your own words. To summarize means to distill only the most essential points of someone else's work. What's more, a summary is normally shorter than a paraphrase of a certain work.

When you begin to summarize a passage, you need first to absorb the meaning of the passage, and then to capture in your own words the most important elements from the original passage.

13.2 The Checklist for Organizing a Summary

— Begin with the name of the author, or the title of the original essay.
— Introduce the controlling idea of the author clearly.
— State briefly the essential supporting points of the author.
— Summarize the main points briefly.
— Paraphrase the author's idea and use quotation marks when quoting.
— Rearrange the summary logically.

Tips:

- Make sure you pick one tense and stick to it. The past tense is the easiest to stick to when you write about a story.
- Make sure that all your sentences can be understood on the first reading.
- Make sure that you haven't left out any important information.
- Make sure that the words you choose to use can genuinely convey your intended meaning. That is, use your dictionary if necessary.

Sample 13-1
Original passage:

The sea turtles, especially the leatherbacks, are undoubtedly one of nature's most amazing creatures. They roam the warm seas of the world throughout their life and come ashore only to lay eggs. Malaysia with its long sandy shorelines has been destined as one of their breeding grounds. Unfortunately, the number of leatherback turtles landing on the beaches has been declining over the years. According to the World Wildlife Fund (WWF) estimates, about 2,000 leatherbacks arrived on Malaysian beaches in 1970. In 1989, only between 30 and 60 leatherbacks were found. The drastic drop within such a short span is certainly a great cause for concern. Where have they gone? Are they avoiding the beaches of Malaysia? Whatever it is, the message is disturbingly clear—they may become an extinct species soon if no concerted effort is taken to check the decline now.

The belief that the declining landings of turtles in Malaysia is the result of increasing landings in other parts of the world is a fallacy. This is because the scenario is the same in other countries known to have been visited by the turtles. What has caused the species to dwindle at such a rapid rate? There are many reasons, but an obvious one is none other than man's greed. As we know, turtles are killed for their meat. In the days before refrigeration, turtles had been a source of fresh food for the sailing ships. Today, turtle soup is a favorite dish among the Asians. Their shells have become coveted items for decorations and jewelry. Their eggs which are meant to be hatched into young turtles, are instead harvested and eaten. When deep sea fishing nets inadvertently trap the turtles, fishermen often kill the turtles instead of cutting their nets to release them. Pollution of the sea has also reduced the number of turtles. Many are choked to death by the plastic bags that they mistake for jelly fish. It appears that the turtles are no longer safe in the sea where they spend most of their lives.

Neither are they safe when the females come ashore to lay eggs. In fact, this is the time when they are particularly vulnerable as their movements are slow on land. The nesting places for these turtles have also been greatly reduced. As more and more beaches are taken over for tourism with the construction of hotels, chalets and condominiums, the breeding grounds are reduced in the process. The intrusion of tourists into these places make it difficult for the turtles to lay their eggs. They have to look elsewhere to places that are still quiet and undisturbed to lay their eggs. Unfortunately these ideal places are few to come by now. Too much development has taken place even along the coastline in most countries.

Perhaps all is not lost yet. Sincere efforts are being taken to check the decline. In Malaysia, it is heartening to note that concrete steps have been taken to protect the turtles that come ashore to lay eggs. The indiscriminate collection of turtle eggs on the beaches is no more allowed. Turtle sanctuaries have been set up in Rantau Abang in Terengganu. The eggs collected by designated officials are sent to hatcheries in the sanctuaries. In this way, the loss of eggs and the rate of mortality among the baby turtles are reduced. In other words, more baby turtles are now able to return to sea and grow into adulthood.

In an effort to discourage the public from eating turtle eggs, a Turtle Enactment Act has been introduced to prohibit the sale of leatherback eggs. The WWF has also launched the "Save the Turtle Campaign" to create an awareness among the public to help save the endangered species. In this way, the consumption of turtle eggs and perhaps turtle meat will be discouraged, thus putting a stop to the illegal sale of eggs and trapping of turtles. Let us hope that it is not too late to save these fascinating creatures from becoming extinct.

Summary:

The declining landings of turtles in Malaysia are due to uncontrolled catching for their meat, shells and eggs. Many are inadvertently caught in deep sea fishing nets. Pollution of the sea has also reduced the number of turtles. Many die of suffocation by discarded plastic bags. Besides, turtles are most vulnerable when they come ashore to lay eggs. Their nesting places have also been reduced due to the development of tourism along the coasts. Nevertheless, concrete steps have been taken to arrest the decline. Indiscriminate collection and sale of turtle eggs are banned. Turtle sanctuaries have been set up, thereby reducing the rate of mortality among the baby turtles. Lastly, an awareness campaign has been launched by WWF to discourage the public from eating turtle eggs. (125 words)

Sample 13-2
Original passage:

I run Green Way International, a conservation group that campaigns against and conducts research into environmental pollution. The data that we receive from all corners of the globe give us no cause for optimism—the results of our studies and the minimal success of our crusades testify to the fact that we are fighting a losing battle.

Of course, environmental pollution is not a modern phenomenon. It began ever since people began to congregate in towns and cities. The ancient Athenians removed refuse to dumps outside the main parts of their cities. The Romans dug trenches outside their cities where they could deposit their garbage, waste and even corpses. These unhygienic practices undoubtedly led to the outbreak of viral diseases.

Unfortunately, man refuses to acknowledge or correct his past mistakes. As cities grew in the Middle Ages, pollution became even more evident. Ordinances had to be passed in medieval cities against indiscriminate dumping of waste into the streets and canals. In sixteenth century England, efforts were made to curb the use of coal to reduce the amount of smoke in the air. These, however, had little effect on the people's consciences.

I think that the Industrial Revolution of the nineteenth century was the point of no return. It heralded the mushrooming of industries and power driven machines. True, the standard of living increased, but it was achieved at a great environmental cost.

In Cubatao of Brazil, for instance, industrial plants belch thousands of tons of pollutants daily and the air contains high levels of benzene, a cancer causing substance. In one recent year alone, I discovered 13,000 cases of respiratory diseases and that a tenth of the workers risked contracting leukemia. Green Way International hoped to seek the assistance of Brazil's government officials, but we were sorely disappointed. Unwilling to lose revenue from the factories, they blamed the high mortality rate on poor sanitation and malnutrition. We continue to provide medical assistance to the inhabitants of Brazil's "Valley of Death," but there is little else that we can do to alleviate the suffering.

Our planet has its own mechanisms to deal with natural pollutants. Decay, sea spray and volcanic eruptions release more sulphur than all the power plants, smelters and industries in the world do. Lightning bolts create nitrogen oxides and trees emit hydrocarbons called terpenes. These substances are cycled through the ecosystem and change form, passing through plant and animal tissues, sink to the sea and return to Earth to begin the cycle all over again.

However, can the earth assimilate the additional millions of tons of chemicals like sulphur, chlorofluorocarbons, carbon dioxide and methane that our industries release each year? If the dying forests in Germany, Eastern Europe, Sweden and Norway give any indication, then the answer must be a resounding "No!." Oxides of sulphur and nitrogen from the power plants and factories and motor vehicles have acidified the soil. This has destroyed the organisms necessary to the nutrient cycle as well as injured the trees' fine root systems. The weakened trees become more vulnerable to drought, frost, fungi and insects.

Many a time, my staff have returned from their research tours around the world, lamenting the slow but sure destruction of our cultural treasures. The carvings on the Parthenon, a magnificent building in Athens, have been eroded by acid deposition. The Roman Colosseum, England's Westminster Abbey and India's Taj Mahal have also fallen victim to insidious chemicals that float in the air. The stained glass windows of cathedrals from the twelfth and thirteenth centuries have been corroded to barely recognizable images as well.

Years earlier, I had studied a secluded island in the Pacific and found its undisturbed ecosystem in complete balance and stability. In despair, I once contemplated living the rest of my days on the island in solitude. Pollution, however, is no respecter of boundaries—when I reached the island, the beaches were awash with trash and dead marine life while the once-lush foliage were sparse and limp. It was then that I realized this dying planet needs allies and not fatalism and resignation. I returned to resume my crusade and I hope others will join me...

Summary:
Pollution has plagued Earth since people established towns and cities. Ancient Athenians and Romans disposed their waste and even corpses in dumps and trenches outside their cities. These indiscriminate practices caused viral outbreaks. In the medieval era, smoke polluted the air, with the increased use of coal. Pollution became even more prevalent following the Industrial Revolution of the nineteenth century. Today, factories and motor vehicles are the main cause of environmental contamination. Toxic gases and chemicals like benzene, sulphur, chlorofluorocarbons, carbon dioxide, methane, nitrogen and mercury oxides are emitted and cause cancer, leukemia and respiratory diseases. These substances have also led to the destruction of flora and fauna. Major artistic and historical relics have been corroded and damaged too. (119 words)

Sample 13-3
Original passage:
Buying things today is so simple. Just enter a shop, say a book store, choose the desired book and pay for it. Long ago, before the invention of money, how did people trade?

The most primitive way of exchange should be the barter trade. In this form of transaction, people used goods to exchange for the things that they had in mind. For instance, if person A wanted a book and he had a spare goat, he must look for someone who had the exact opposite, that is, that someone, say person B, must have a spare book of person A's choice and be also in need of a goat. When such a person is found, the problem does not end here. A big goat may be worth not only one book, hence person B may have to offer person A something else, say five chickens. However, he runs the risk of person A rejecting the offer as he may not need the chickens. The above example clearly illustrates the inefficiency of barter trading.

Many years later, the cumbersome barter trade finally gave way to the monetary form of exchange when the idea of money was invented. In the early days, almost anything could qualify as money: beads, shells and even fishing hooks. Then in a region near Turkey, gold coins were used as money. In the beginning, each coin had a different denomination. It was only later, in about 700 BC, that Gyges, the king of Lydia, standardized the value of each coin and even printed his name on the coins.

Monetary means of transaction at first beat the traditional barter trade. However, as time went by, the thought of carrying a ponderous pouch of coins for shopping appeared not only troublesome but thieves attracting. Hence, the Greek and Roman traders who bought goods from people in faraway cities, invented checks to solve the problem. Not only are paper checks easy to carry around, they discouraged robbery as these checks can only be used by the person whose name is printed on the notes. Following this idea, banks later issued notes in exchange for gold deposited with them. These bank notes can then be used as cash. Finally, governments of today adopted the idea and began to print paper money, backed by gold for the country's use.

Today, besides enjoying the convenience of using paper notes as the mode of exchange, technology has led men to invent other means of transaction, too, like the credit and cash cards.

Summary:

Long ago, people bought things through barter trade. However, the difficulty of having to look for the right partner and dividing the goods led people to switch over to monetary transaction. At first, beads, shells and fishing hooks were used as money. Near Turkey, gold coins with irregular denominations were used for trade. Later, King Gyges standardized the individual coin value. People soon found carrying coins around for shopping troublesome and thieves courting. Hence, merchants started to issue checks with names of the users on them to discourage robbery. Following that, banks started to issue cash notes in return for gold deposited with them. Finally, adopting the idea, today, governments printed paper money backed by gold for the country's usage. (119 words)

Sample 13-4
Original passage:

Are you having problems feeling sleepy when you want to be alert and *vice-versa*? Perhaps you need to look at your diet, as it may be the culprit. The brain's state of sleepiness or alertness, calmness or anxiousness, is said to be determined by messengers in the body called neuro-transmitters.

One of these which is called serotonin helps us feel calm and relaxed. Researchers have found that eating large amounts of carbohydrate foods, such as sweets, potatoes and grain products increases brain levels of serotonin. High-protein meals or snacks, consisting mostly of meat, on the other hand, tend to cause brain levels of serotonin to remain low.

A French study that varied the amount of carbohydrate fed to subjects found that an intake of carbohydrate with an equal serving of protein products did not cause drowsiness. But when very large amounts of carbohydrate were provided without protein, subjects reported feeling drowsy. This drowsiness occurred even after exercise which normally causes people to feel more alert.

We can take advantage of these findings to determine when to stay alert or to get some sleep. A snack that is largely carbohydrate-based may relax us and make it easier for us to fall asleep. On the other hand, when you are trying to stay awake, a balanced meal that includes protein (meat, chicken, fish, dairy products or dried beans) as well as modest portions of grains, vegetables and fruit is more likely to help than loading up on a huge platter of meatless pasta.

Some experiments suggest that the effects may vary depending on the particular carbohydrate foods chosen. The ability of carbohydrates to increase brain serotonin involves a rise in insulin levels in the blood when carbohydrate is eaten. Large carbohydrate portions, or those that cause a faster rise in blood sugar such as sweets, potatoes, bread, refined cereals will cause greater increases in serotonin (and sleepiness). Fruit and dried beans contain carbohydrate that raises blood sugar more slowly, and so would not be expected to raise serotonin levels as high.

But what about good nutrition? Eating to stay alert just means including some protein in our meals. However, do not overeat grain products just because they are fat-free. By including plenty of high-fiber fruit or vegetables in meals, blood sugar and insulin will rise moderately, and serotonin level in the brain will not jump dramatically.

Nevertheless, when it comes to getting a good night's sleep, studies clearly show that it is more than just what we eat. Some people are very sensitive to caffeine in coffee, tannin in tea and even to soda pops, even when it is consumed as early as 5:00 p.m. Other people find that the key to a good night's sleep lies in establishing a routine pattern of pre-bedtime behaviors, keeping a consistent bedtime, getting regular exercise and learning relaxation techniques. If you are extremely sleepy throughout the day, check your eating patterns. Do not try to compensate for lack of sleep at night by eating protein and scraping by on caffeine; adequate sleep is essential.

Summary:

Carbohydrates contain serotonin which helps make us feel calm and relaxed. Consuming large amounts of carbohydrates causes drowsiness as they make us feel relaxed. However, if we want to stay alert, we should consume a balanced meal containing protein and carbohydrates. Research suggests that carbohydrates increase brain serotonin leading to a rise in insulin levels in the blood. Therefore, a correct diet helps in keeping us alert as the blood sugar, serotonin and insulin levels rise only moderately. Getting enough sleep is also necessary and to some people, it means having an adequate established routine before going to bed. (99 words)

Sample 13-5

Original passage:

Vitamin A is found only in yellow animal fats, in egg-yolk, milk and cheese. It is particularly plentiful in fish-liver oil, hence fish-liver oil is used for preventing and curing illness caused by lack of vitamin A. In a well-fed, healthy human being, the liver can store up sufficient vitamin A to meet the body's requirements for six months.

Although vitamin A itself is not present in plants, many plants produce a substance called carotene, formed from leaf-green which our bodies can convert into vitamin A. Carotene is the yellowish-red coloring matter in carrots. The greener a leaf is, the more carotene it usually contains. Hence the importance of green, leafy vegetables in the diet as a source of carotene. Tomatoes, papayas, mangoes and bananas contain more carotene than most other fruits. Red palm oil contains so much carotene that it is used instead of cod-liver oil. Thus, it is very valuable, both as a food-fat and for deep-frying.

Vitamin A and carotene are insoluble in water and they are not destroyed by heat unless oxygen is present. Boiling in water, therefore, does not destroy much vitamin A or carotene.

Vitamin A encourages healthy growth and physical fitness. Young animals soon stop growing and die if vitamin A is not present in their diet. This vitamin keeps the moist surfaces lining the digestive canal, the lungs and air passages healthy. It also helps keep the ducts of the various glands, the tissue that lines the eyelids and covers the front of the eyeball functional. As vitamin A helps these tissues build up resistance to infection, it is often called the anti-infective vitamin.

Some of the most common disorders in people are caused by a shortage of vitamin A, when the moist tissues become dry and rough. This often causes serious eye diseases, followed by infection of the air-passages. The skin may also become flaky and rough. Another defect caused by shortage of vitamin A is "night-blindness," when the affected person has distinct vision only in bright light.

As the body cannot produce vitamin A, it has to come from external sources. Thus a well-balanced diet is required and is usually sufficient to provide the necessary amount. There is, therefore, no need to supplement the need in the form of pills.

Summary:

Vitamin A is found only in certain food substances. It is also abundant in fish-liver oil. Our liver is able to store some vitamin A to meet our requirements. Carotene is a substance which our bodies can convert into vitamin A. It is found in green leafy vegetables, carrots and some fruits. Vitamin A is not easily destroyed by heat. It is essential for healthy growth and physical fitness. It also helps keep the eyes from infection. A lack of vitamin A could lead to eye diseases and skin disorders. Thus, a well-balanced diet is needed to ensure that the body receives the necessary supply of vitamin! It is not necessary to take extra supplements. (116 words)

Sample 13-6
Original passage:

We are bombarded by many advertisements every day. Vendors try all means and ways to gain our attention and sell us their products or services. Advertisements appear everywhere—on television programs, radios, in the papers, magazines, pamphlets and so on.

Advertisements are actually very useful, though we sometimes feel annoyed when they interrupt our favorite television programs. They provide us with free information on the products and services. There are two types of advertisements. The informative advertisements are the ones which provide us with the details of the products or services. This information is especially useful if the product or service is new. For instance, when we need to buy a computer, advertisements describing the latest models and their different functions would be extremely helpful. However, only a minority of the advertisements are informative ones. Many of them belong to the second category—the persuasive kind. These advertisements not only tell us more about the products, at the same time, they persuade customers to buy them by claiming that their products are superior to the rivalry ones. These claims may sometimes be untrue.

Besides being informative and persuasive, advertisements also help to subsidize the prices of magazines and newspapers. Our newspapers are sold at a low price of about one dollar, owing to the advertisements in the papers; otherwise, the price would have been higher.

While advertisements can be good helpers for shopping, they do have their shortcomings. Most advertisements aim to sell only. Faults of the products or services are usually hidden from the consumers. Hence, sometimes we feel deceived if the product or service we bought does not turn out the way the advertisements claim to be.

Sometimes, advertisements by rival competitors can get very intensive, especially when there are many firms producing similar products. One common example is the washing powder. There are so many advertisements for the different brands that customers sometimes get confused over what they should buy. Furthermore, having more advertisements would mean that the production cost of the firm would be increased. These rises in cost are usually passed on to the consumers in the form of higher prices.

Hence, in conclusion, though I do advocate advertisements, I do not deny their flaws. Without them, we might have to buy things based on incomplete information or go through more complicated ways before getting to know the products or services. On the other hand, too many advertisements also complicate our buying decisions. So I would say that we cannot live without advertisements but we must be careful how we live with them.

Summary:

There are two types of advertisements. Informative advertisements provide consumers with information about the products or services. They are especially useful when we are purchasing new products. The second kind is the persuasive ones which provide us with products information and also persuade us to buy them by claiming the superiority of their products. Advertisements also benefit readers of newspapers and magazines by helping to subsidize the prices. One disadvantage of advertisements is that they sometimes aim to sell only and cover up the flaws of the advertised products. Consumers may sometimes get confused over buying decisions when too many advertisements are presented. Advertising also raises the production costs which in turn increases the prices of the products, too. (120 words)

Chapter Fourteen
Abstract Writing

14.1　What Is an Abstract?

An abstract should be viewed as a miniature version of the paper. The abstract should provide a brief summary of each of the main sections of the paper: Introduction, Literature Review, Research Methodology, Results and Discussion. As Houghton (1975) put it, "An abstract can be defined as a summary of the information in a document." "A well-prepared abstract enables readers to identify the basic content of a document quickly and accurately, to determine its relevance to their interests, and thus to decide whether they need to read the document in its entirety" (American National Standards Institute, 1979).

14.2　Some Conventions of Abstract Writing

Usually an abstract should not exceed 250 words and should be designed to define clearly what is dealt with in the paper. The abstract should be typed as a single paragraph.

The Abstract should

(1) State the principal objectives and scope of the investigation;

(2) Describe the methods employed;

(3) Summarize the results;

(4) State the principal conclusions.

Tips:

● When writing the abstract, examine every word carefully. If you can tell your story in 100 words, do not use 200.

● Most abstracts should be written in the past tense, because it refers to work done.

> • The abstract should never give any information or conclusion that is not stated in the paper.
> • References to the literature must not be cited in the abstract (except in rare instances, such as modification of a previously published method). Likewise, the abstract should not include or refer to tables and figures.

14.3 Different Types of Abstract

1. Informative abstract

An informative abstract is designed to condense the paper. It can and should briefly state the problem, the method used to study the problem and the principal data and conclusions. Often, the abstract supplants the need for reading the full paper; without such abstracts, scientists would not be able to keep up in active areas of research. This is the type of abstract that is used as a "heading" in most journals today.

2. Indicative abstract

Another common type of abstract is the indicative abstract (sometimes called a descriptive abstract). This type of abstract is designed to indicate the subjects dealt with in a paper, making it easy for potential readers to decide whether to read the paper. However, because of its descriptive rather than substantive nature, it can seldom serve as a substitute for the full paper. Thus, indicative abstracts should not be used as "heading" abstracts in research papers, but they may be used in other types of publications (review papers, conference reports, the government report literature, etc.); such indicative abstracts are often of great value to reference librarians.

3. Informative- indicative abstract

An informative-indicative abstract is a combined form that bears specific information about the principal findings and results and general information about the rest of the document. This type of abstract offers fewer details, instead, giving emphasis to the author's chief contribution.

14.4 The Formalized Structure of Abstract

An abstract usually consists of the following three major parts:
(1) Topic sentence.
(2) Supporting sentences.
(3) Concluding sentences.

14.4.1 Topic sentence

The first sentence in an abstract is usually called the "topic sentence." By answering the question of "what," the topic sentence always goes straightforwardly to the subject or the problem and indicates the primary objectives of the paper.

Examples:
- The purpose of this paper is…
- The primary goal of this research is…
- The intention of this paper is to survey…
- The overall objective of this study is…
- In this paper, we aim at…
- Our goal has been to provide…
- The chief aim of the present work is to investigate the features of…
- The authors are now initiating some experimental investigation to establish…
- The work presented in this paper focuses on several aspects of the following…
- The problem we have outlined deals largely with the study of…
- With his many years' research, the author's endeavor is to explain why…
- The primary object of this fundamental research will be to reveal the cause of…
- The main objective of our investigation has been to obtain some knowledge of…
- With recent research, the author intends to outline the framework of…
- The author attempted the set of experiments with a view to demonstrating certain phenomena…
- The experiment being made by our research group is aimed at obtaining the result of…
- The main objective of our investigation has been to obtain some knowledge of…
- Experiments on… were made in order to measure the amount of…
- The emphasis of this study lies in…

14.4.2 Supporting sentences

The topic sentence is usually followed by more than one supporting sentence which further specifies the subject to be presented. Research methods, experiments, procedures, investigations, calculations, analyses, results and other significant information items will be provided in this part.

Examples:
- The method used in our study is known as…
- The technique we applied is referred to…
- The procedure they followed can be briefly described as…
- The approach adopted extensively is called…
- Detailed information has been acquired by the authors using…
- The research has recorded valuable data using the newly-developed method…
- This is a working theory which is based on the idea that…
- The fundamental feature of this theory is as follows…

- The theory is characterized by…
- The experiment consisted of three steps, which are described in…

14.4.3 Concluding sentences

As the ending part of an abstract, concluding sentences usually analyze the results, explain the application and point out the significance of the research.

Examples:

- In conclusion, we state that…
- To sum up, it may be stated that…
- It is concluded that…
- The results of the experiment indicate that…
- The studies we have performed showed that…
- The pioneer studies that the authors attempted have indicated in…
- We carried out several studies which have demonstrated that….
- The research we have done suggests that…
- The investigation carried out by… has revealed that…
- Laboratory studies of… did not furnish any information about…
- All our preliminary results throw light on the nature of…

Useful expressions for abstract writing

report; show; demonstrate; model; indicate; suggest; propose; imply; reveal; present; discuss; describe; examine; measure; identify; infer; deal with; cope with; be concerned with; represent; estimate; analyze/make an analysis; distinguish; observe; obtain agreement; combine; compare; differ; differ from/with/in; make a difference; conclude; draw/make a conclusion; sum up; conduct research on; investigate; make an investigation; survey; apply; employ; use; constitute; fulfill the gap; fulfill the role; perform a crucial function/role; construct; make/carry out/perform an experiment in; experiment on/with; experimentally; fabricate; test this hypothesis by; performed normally; require; determine; quantify; measure; replicate; discover; identify; find; findings; results

Sample 14-1

This project involves discovering how the American Revolution was remembered during the nineteenth century. The goal is to show that the American Revolution was memorialized by the actions of the United States government during the 1800s. This has been done by examining events such as the Supreme Court cases of John Marshall and the Nullification Crisis. Upon examination of these events, it becomes clear that John Marshall and John Calhoun (creator of the Doctrine of Nullification) attempted to use the American Revolution to bolster their claims by citing speeches from Founding Fathers. Through showing that the American Revolution lives on in memory, this research highlights the importance of the revolution in shaping the actions of the United States government (from "The Commemoration and Memorialization of the American Revolution").

Sample 14-2

The purpose of this research is to identify a subtype of autism called Developmental Verbal Dyspraxia (DVD). DVD is a motor-speech problem, disabling oral-motor movements needed for speaking. The first phase of the project involves a screening interview where we identify DVD and Non-DVD kids. We also use home videos to validate answers on the screening interview. The final phase involves home visits where we use several assessments to confirm the child's diagnosis and examine the connection between manual and oral motor challenges. By identifying DVD as a subtype of autism, we will eliminate the assumption that all autistics have the same characteristics. This will allow for more individual consideration of autistic people and may direct future research on the genetic factors in autism (from "Subtype of Autism: Developmental Verbal Dyspraxia").

Sample 14-3

The study is to show how even a "sport" video game can incorporate many types of learning, to call attention to what might be overlooked as significant forms of learning, and to understand and take advantage of the opportunities video games afford as more deliberate learning environments. The aspects explored are the skills and techniques required to be successful in the game, the environment that skaters skate in, the personal vs. group identity that is shown through the general appearance of the skater, and the values and icons that the game teaches players. We are finding that sport video games support learning; we hope to find how one learns about oneself as a learner from playing (from "The Tony Hawk Learning Project").

Sample 14-4

The Latitudinal Defense Hypothesis predicts that levels of defense are the highest near the equator and decrease toward the poles. This hypothesis is based mainly on insect herbivory that occurs during the summer. Mammilian herbivory in winter is a more likely driver of plant defense levels in northern latitudes. Early successional trees such as birches are favored by fire and provide an important food source for mammals like snowshoe hares. In order to test the Latitudinal Defense Hypothesis, we collected birch seeds from eight locations in northwestern Canada and grew seedlings in a common garden. We assessed levels of defense by counting resin glands because resin glands are negatively correlated with snowshoe hare preference. This research will provide valuable information regarding the biogeography of defense and address the role of fire in plant-mammal interactions on a continental scale (from "Biogeography of Chemical Defense in Birch Trees").

Sample 14-5

Each day 14,000 people become infected with HIV/AIDS, making the development of an effective vaccine one of the world's top public health priorities. David Watkins' laboratory is attempting to develop HIV vaccines that elicit cellular immune responses utilizing the simian immunodeficiency virus (SIV)-infected rhesus macaque animal model. A major component of the cell-mediated immune response is cytotoxic T-lymphocytes (CTL). It is thought that CTL plays an important role in controlling HIV and SIV. Most standard immunological assays do not measure antiviral activity directly, limiting our understanding of CTL effectiveness. To address this, the Watkins laboratory developed a novel neutralization assay that quantifies the ability of virus-specific CTL populations to control viral growth. Evaluating the antiviral activity of CTL of different specificities will identify those CTL most effective against SIV. This information will likely impact the design of future HIV vaccines (from "Understanding Cell-Mediated Immune Responses Against Simian Immunodeficiency Virus").

Sample 14-6

The purpose of this study is to identify relationships between the physical and genetic characteristics of bones in mice. The physical characteristics include size, density and the force required to break the bone, while the genetic ones are the genes of the marker loci associated with the genes that affect these qualities. This study uses strains of mice with reduced genetic variation. The two strains of mice that are the most phenotypically extreme, meaning those with the strongest and weakest bones, are crossed. The F2 generation from that cross is then analyzed. The results of this analysis can be used to find which genotypes correlate with specific bone properties like size, density and failure load. The anticipated outcome of this lab is the identification of the genotypes that affect bone strength in mice. The findings may be useful in treating medical conditions that are related to bone strength (from "The Genetics of Bone Strength in Mice").

Sample 14-7

Upon receiving the Wisconsin Idea Undergraduate Fellowship, the summer and fall 2003 semesters were spent designing and implementing a Hmong Political Council, Inc. (HPC). The fellowship addressed the immediate need felt by our local government and the Hmong refugee community to develop a political voice expressing the economic, political and social needs of the Hmong refugee community. It was implemented through the collaboration of the United Refugee Services of Wisconsin, Professor Macken, the Hmong community and myself. Extensive research was conducted at the local, state and national level involving the studying of IRS requirements, lobbying rights, other political councils and the needs of the Wisconsin Hmong community. HPC is now a legal non-profit organization that has held two fundraisers, released press statements, and worked with State and National political figures to address the needs of the Hmong community.

Within the year, HPC plans to be lobbying at the state level (from "Southeast Asian Political Action Committee: Democracy at Work!").

Sample 14-8
"Fostering H.O.P.E.: Helping Overcome Poverty through Education for Teen Moms"

This program was designed to address the prevalent issues of teen parenthood and poverty. The idea was to introduce and reinforce the importance of obtaining a post secondary education to teen mothers in their junior or senior year of high school. The program ran for eight weeks during the summer of 2003. Participants met once a week to participate in group building activities, get insights to what it will take to finish school and receive information on services that are available to help them along the way. The young women also had the opportunity to tour the UW and MATC campuses. The participants walked away from the program with a sense of hope that they are able to pursue their dreams despite their difficult situations.

Sample 14-9
"Blind Construction: Mixed Media"

The basis of this project was to create a garment using mixed media in order to mimic the human body. The materials we used to create this piece include: buckram, copper wire, spray paint, fabric paint, a variety of novelty fabrics and chains. The techniques we created in order to manipulate the piece include: fabric branding and burning, grid painting, sewing, draping, molding buckram, and coiling. Our overall approach was to create a theatrical wearable art piece. Upon completion of the assignment we found the piece aesthetically pleasing because of the way it molds to the human body, but can be a piece all on its own.

Chapter Fifteen
Writing for Delivery

Introduction

Reports and seminars, presentations, as well as public speaking are written work commonly applied in daily writings, such as in newspapers, office services, before/after or even in the course of a project, evaluation of one's work at school or in some particular activities. Reports are mainly in written form providing the information and situations and answer the questions required. This chapter introduces reports, seminars, proposals, presentations and public speech, including their features and differences as well as some skills concerning how to manage a good writing of reports, presentations, public speech, etc.

15.1 Report

Report is a written or spoken description of a situation or event and its definitions vary due to its uses:

- A description giving people information they need, or an account of something, usually followed by "*of, on, about* ";
- A piece of writing in a newspaper about something that is happening, or part of a new program, followed by "*on, of*";
- An official argument that carefully considers a particular subject, followed by "*on*";
- Information that tells something happened, which may or may not be true, followed by "*of*";
- [BrE] A written statement by teachers about children's work at school, which is sent to his or her parents, also called report card in the USA.

15.1.1 Different types of report

Reports can be divided by their functions, such as:

1. Expense report

Sorts of public statement of performing duties, sales, attending meetings, someone's arrival for duty (that is, to report that someone has arrived and is ready for work), etc.;

2. Feasibility/analysis report

Evaluations of data to determine future production;

3. Field report

Analysis of data to determine action, service cost, claim damages;

4. Incident/investigative report

Facts or claims usually telling police or someone in authority that crimes and accidents happened (including someone missing, injured, etc.);

5. Lab/test report

Results of experiments commonly applied in college, university/ institute study and lab research;

6. Periodical/progress report

The report on the job or work, telling people what is happening or what you are going to do as part of your work or of a project.

Sample 15-1-1-1: Evaluation report

Dr Li Xia has worked very hard on different papers, in particular on the joint paper that we are hoping to publish together in the VIGO International Journal of Applied Linguistics. She has also actively taken part in the Second Language Acquisition Reading group as well as seminars of the Institute of Education and the Centre for Literacy and Multilingualism. In addition, she has given me excellent support in the data collection for a research project on the development of an English-Malay vocabulary test. Dr Li Xia is a very talented researcher and I have very much enjoyed working with her over the past year. I would be delighted if Dr Li Xia was able to stay at the University of ×× for another year to continue her research together with me and other colleagues in the Centre for Literacy and Multilingualism.

(Signature) ×××
December 11, 2013

Sample 15-1-1-2: Investigative report

INCIDENT INVESTIGATION REPORT	XXX LIMITED		
Department: Mines	Date & Time: 10.08.08 / 3:00 PM	Location: Near W/S & Thd. Triangle	
Brief of incident: Explosive Van Helper got minor injury on his forehead			
Name of reporter:	Designation:	Type of injury / loss (if any):	
XYZ	Explosive Van Helper	Bruise on forehead	

continued

Company's Employee/Contractors' Employee: ABC & Co. Contractor's employee					
Type of Incident (place tick mark(s) √ in the applicable fields)					
First Aid Case		Fatality		Unsafe Act	
Medical Treatment Case (in house)	√	Lost Work Day Case		Unsafe Condition	√
Referral Case (Out Station Hospital)		Restricted Workday Case	√	Unauthorized Entry Case	
Occupational Illness		No Injury Case		Outside Premises Case	
Cause(s) of Incident or Condition					
Lack of Attention	√	Poor Housekeeping	√	Lack of Safety Work Permit	
Failure to Follow Proper Procedure	√	No Written Procedure	√	Proper PPE not Used	√
Lack of Communication		Congested Area		Hazards not Identified	√
Unfamiliar with the Equipment		Improper Design		Improper Maintenance	
Unfamiliar with Operating Procedure		Improper Equipment		Insufficient Training	√
Carelessness	√	Improper Installation		Use of Alcohol	
Any Other (Please Specify) :					
Description of Incident : While explosives Van was going to the AN Storage site, the front wheel of the explosive Van fell into a ditch formed on the road due to rain water. Mr. XYZ, helper, who was sitting relaxed in the Van, got alerted from the jerk, hardly managed to balance his body and escaped from a fall from his seat. He got small injury (Bruise) on the forehead.					
Key Witnesses Interviewed:					

Name	Detail of Input
Mr. ABC, Driver of the Van	The road to Mines got flooded with rain water 2 days ago. Being in hurry, he could not see the ditch merged into water. Felt a jerk & helper struck with dashboard.
Mr. ZZZ, Shift Engr.	Heavy rainfall during last 2 days. Road repairing hampered due to Motor Grader being under B/D. Dozer engaged at Hill # 8. Speed of the Van was 30 kmph.

Observations & Findings: (1) The speed of the Van was greater than the prescribed speed of 10 kmph on flooded mines roads. (2) There is no provision of safety belt in the Van for the helper. (3) No alternative arrangement, such as manual road repairing at critical locations while the machine is under B/D. (4)

Root Cause / Probable Cause(s) of Incident: (1) High speed driving in the restricted area; (2) No provision of seat belt for helper; (3) Non identification of such hazards & lack of written procedure & training to driver & helper

Recommendations for Corrective & Preventive Action(s):

No.	Recommendation	Action by	Target Date	Closing Date	Closed by
1.	The approach road to the AN storage and other mines roads should be repaired by filling up the ditches formed as a result of surface runoff.	XXX	dd /mm/yy	dd/mm/yy	XXX
2.	Risk Metrics to be thoroughly reviewed & awareness be provided to the operators on the precautions to be taken while driving, in particular, during monsoon.	YYY	dd/mm/yy	dd/mm/yy	YYY

continued

No.	Recommendation	Action by	Target Date	Closing Date	Closed by
3.	All the seats in vehicles running in the mines must be provided with seat belts.	WWW	dd/mm/yy	dd/mm/yy	WWW
Preventive Action(s): Above actions to be simultaneously implemented in ×××××× Mine by HOD (Mines)					
Investigation Team Leader & Members Date: / /					
Name	Signature	Name	Signature	Name	Signature	Name	Signature
A		B		C		C	
Copy distributed to: HOD (Mines), I/C Training, Contractor, Victim, Safety Cell, Quality Cell & Factory Manager					

When writing a report, remember the following tips:
- Use accurate materials;
- Develop facts logically;
- Set a new paragraph for each subject or stage;
- Write in a plain and efficient style.

15.1.2 Reading a report

Reading reports is applied in study and research, and also in some daily communications. Reading reports may include some sections as follows:

- Brief introduction of the author, the time of the work published, and when needed, the event or background of the readings and the publishing house and time as well.

- Gist of the readings/story: (Like an abstract in writing style) To be complete, objective; in present tense for a story and the original tense for non-fiction readings, such as, past tense for a history and present/simple future one for a science fiction, etc.

- Comment: The essential section of the report. It is the reporter's view on the readings: merits/worthiness and pros and cons and the impacts on the present and the future, etc.

Sample 15-1-2-1: Article review comments

Review comments on "Can classroom learners use statistical learning?
A new perspective on motion event construal in a second language"

This paper presents an interesting approach to motion event construal in a second language. The experimental procedure has been followed with rigour and excellent methodology. Data from corpuses of English and Chinese and oral narratives in L1 English, L1 Chinese and L2 English from Chinese students have been analysed. It is an interesting contribution to the field since: i) there is a novelty on the application of statistical learning to motion events, and ii) the use of Chinese and English as the languages of the study.

However, the typological differences between these languages and the languages in the study by XX and XX (under review) should be taken into consideration. The authors claim that classroom learners can adjust the frequency which they use L2 verbs to that of native speakers, but are less successful in doing this than those who had been exposed to the target language during a year. This conclusion is based on the comparison of two different studies involving two different L2s and two different typological relations L1-L2 (English＞French, Chinese＞English). I think these conclusions should be revisited and mitigated.

Apart from this, it would be interesting to give a brief explanation of how the findings of the study can be used in the classroom to facilitate the mappings onto the L2, especially for those students who have to learn the language in the classroom environment. In other words, if the answer to the question of the title is "yes," it would be interesting to know more about "how."

I consider this paper should be accepted, taking these comments into consideration and following some revision specified below.

15.2 Proposal

Proposals are plans or suggestions made formally to an official person or group, for example, the government's proposal for the regulation of the industry and the proposal to reduce the traffic accident. Proposals, like reports, should include some data and statements to make clear the situation. Nevertheless, proposals allow you to state your assumption of the consequence or the results.

A proposal will contain:

1. Introduction
Usually, a statement of the objective and advantages when the proposal is taken.

2. Problem/background
Details of the existing problem and the urgency of a new plan.

3. Proposal/solution
All of the particulars, such as procedures, methods, capabilities, costs, personnel and action schedules, sometimes with separate headings.

4. Consequences
Assumption of advantages/disadvantages.

5. Conclusions
A call to actions/set of recommendations.

Proposals can use various delivery media, such as letter, fax, e-mail, etc.

Sample 15-2-1: A salesperson who works for a company renting office space has faxed the proposal below to a client

Dear Mr. Rice,

Thank you for your order by fax. Further to your request for office space for twelve months, I would like to mention that I can also offer you a 10% discount for bookings of an eighteen-month period.

You enquired about the availability at the Virginia Walk Centre and offices are still vacant. However, please note that there is limited parking and some offices are on different floors. As an interesting alternative, you might wish to consider a new premise called Dockside (about one mile down riverside from Virginia Walk). It has the following features:

1. A first-floor open-plan office space (75 m^2) with wonderful views of the old harbour.

2. A convenient three-minute walk from the station and ideal for cyclists with a path along the riverside.

3. Suitable parking facilities for over twenty staff.

Please consider this possibility and the discount would still apply. A visit to the premises can be arranged, although I would suggest a prompt decision on this second option.

I look forward to hearing from you in the very near future.

Yours sincerely,

Hugo Jones

Ex. 15-2-1

Directions: *Write a proposal for investment on Sungreen Power Company, a company of solar energy.*

15.3　Seminar

A seminar is a discussion organized by the speaker with the focus around the presentation of an argument or point of view. It is not a debate, but a collaborative forum, delivered in the way of a public speaking, but often promotes a face-to-face discussion at the end. It is relatively informal, at least compared to the lecture systems of academic instructions. Similar to report and public speaking, it should include all the necessary details to give evidence and arguments to the point.

Some other features are as follows:

- A topic selected freely and then narrowed to a specific issue or problem;
- A wide-ranging working bibliography relevant to the focused issue;
- Research questions for the direction of the seminar;
- Preparatory reading is an essential part of the base of the ice-burg—your presentation is 1/10 above the water;

- An organized collection of notes as essential for a seminar as it is for a research paper;
- Proper answers to the problem; and
- Clarified structure and style.

Suggestions for the delivery, which also goes for public speaking
- Use precise, formal language;
- Choose your words carefully;
- Articulate clearly and fluently;
- Vary the volume/tone of your voice;
- Vary the pace of your delivery;
- Maintain eye contact with the audience;
- Stand or sit erect;
- Pause occasionally for emphasis;
- Use humor sparingly;
- Be enthusiastic;
- Breathe naturally;
- Dress appropriately;
- Avoid excessive hand gestures;
- Conclude with confidence.

Prepare a handout including the following items
- Title/purpose/research question;
- Thesis/argument/point of view;
- Outline of major sections;
- Text readings/additional readings;
- Issues and questions for discussion.

Don'ts in seminars

- Don't write or type a rough copy: All you need is a Point-form Outline based on extensive research and careful thought that will certainly enable you to communicate your thesis clearly.

- Don't hold cue cards/index with points: Because the audience may get bored when speakers turn over their cards one by one.

- Don't dominate the discussion: Although the task to conduct a discussion is demanding and rewarding, the sponsor will take the responsibility for sustaining the discussion, and allow you to listen and make brief notes.

Usually, you have to leave 10-15 minutes for the questions, if you have about an hour delivery. At all costs, avoid attempting to monopolize a seminar discussion.

15.4 Presentation

A presentation is the process of presenting a topic to an audience. It is typically a demonstration, lecture or speech meant to inform, persuade or build good will. Visual aids such as PowerPoint or a flipchart can be extremely helpful.

When you organize the structure, you will have:

- **The opening**

Set the scene, provide the background. Give your name and the title of the presentation. Get their attention. Tell them what you are going to do.

- **The middle**

Get into more details; give an outline and analysis of the topic.

- **The ending**

Provide findings or solutions, summarize and conclude, repeat key messages and provide a resolution.

Key principles for developing the structure of a presentation

- Develop an effective strategy to research your content;
- Select examples as you go;
- Be very clear about what the presentation is about;
- Choose the best way to organize the structure for your audience;
- Ensure that there are sufficient links between the sections;
- Ensure that you have a very strong ending.

15.5 Viva

A viva is where you present an overview of your research to a panel and then answer some questions at a more detailed level. You are expected to give a brief outline of the research aims and objectives and the methods used. However, the main part of the presentation should concentrate on the results, conclusions and recommendations.

Viva presentation

The presentation layout	Oral presentation about my dissertation on organizational culture	Timing
	My name Title of my dissertation	2 minutes
	Part I	5 minutes
Introduction: research aims and objectives (Chapter 1)	Introduction to the research including aims/objectives and value of the research justification and scope	

continued

The presentation layout	Oral presentation about my dissertation on organizational culture	Timing
Methods used (Chapter 2)	Background especially on my case study organization. How I undertook the project—methods used issues arising from methods undertaken.	
	Part II	10 minutes
Literature review (Chapter 3)	Literature review	
Data collection (Chapter 4)	Interviews inside case study organization (provide a few useful quotations)	
	Part III	10 minutes
Analysis and discussion (Chapter 5)	Analysis and discussion	
Conclusions	Conclusions	
Recommendations	Recommendations	
	Questions please	10 minutes
Bibliography	Watch out for questions about observation. Did I do it properly?	
	Total timing	37 minutes

15.6 Public Speech

There are occasions where you may find you are expected to speak at a public gathering or social event, and being prepared will require you to plan and prepare the text for this. Here are some steps and tips to help you plan and write a great speech.

The basics that you need to do:

- Choose your topic;
- Find your purpose;
- Get organized;
- Be prepared to be persuasive.

In order that your speech achieves its purpose and has its full effect during the delivery, it should be well organized, which usually contains the opening, the body and the closing.

Five ways to start a speech:

- Refer directly to the subject of your talk;
- Begin with a story or illustration;
- Establish a common bond with the audience;
- Pay an honest compliment to the audience;
- Use humor that steers your audience to the subject.

After the opening, provide the "thesis" or main idea of the speech. Notice that the thesis statement can do three things:

- It tells your audience what kind of speech to expect—an informational speech, a persuasive speech or a humorous speech.
- It sets the tone of your presentation—manner-of-fact, enthusiastic, light-hearted or somber.
- It contains a hint, a seed, a suggestion, or even a direct statement of how the speaker intends to proceed.

The body of the speech will always be the largest part of your speech. The best way to set out the body of your speech is to formulate a series of points that you would like to raise. The points should be organized so that related points follow one after another so that each point builds upon the previous one. This will also give your speech a more logical progression, and make the job of the listener a far easier one. Don't try to overwhelm your audience with mountains of points. It is better to make a small number of points well which is better than to have too many points, none of which are made satisfactorily.

The closing of the speech must contain some of the strongest material. Ways to end a speech:

- End with a brief story that illustrates your main point;
- End with a quotation or ringing phrase;
- Conclude with a poem;
- End with an example of your theme;
- Summarize your main ideas.

Sample 15-6-1: Political speech

If you are sitting here at town hall tonight, it means you want answers. You're here on your own time because you care about this town—and you want to make sure I care about it as much as you do. You want to make sure I'll bring real solutions with me to office, not just bandages. Well, I'm not going to waste any of your time. My main focus today is your children.

"Children are our future." It's a phrase we hear often, but is often used without a full understanding of the implications. "Children are our future" means that children are our priority. Right now, we have some of the lowest test scores in the entire county. Not only that, our math and science scores were around 20 points lower than the state average. That is not making children our priority. That is not securing their future or the future of this town. No one wants to move to a town or stay in a town that has, to be frank, a lousy public education system.

When I was a child here, our town was actually renowned for its stellar schools, so what changed over the last thirty years? For one thing, an exorbitantly high percentage of the town's budget has been allocated to parks, recreation and beautification. Not to say that money was wasted—we have an extraordinarily gorgeous town—but pristine streets won't help our students compete at a national level when it comes to picking a college.

On top of that, we have a staff that is rife with teachers who have been offered tenure despite a long track record of under-performing students. During my time as superintendent of schools 10 years ago, I tried to push for a merit-based tenureship. It didn't go through and I've been pushing ever since. I think the most valuable change we can make as a town is ensuring that our teaching staff is filled with individuals who strive for perfection rather than setting for what's merely acceptable. And what is the better way to motivate our schools than to give them a more appropriate budget? More money invested in our schools means a lower student-to-teacher ratio, which means students will be getting the attention they need and will have a better chance of fulfilling their true potential.

The office of the Mayor should be held by an individual who actually brings solutions that will change the town for the better. This town needs a drastic new approach before it's too late. If we do things the way that they've always been done, then things will remain the way that they've always been. And that, at this point, means a continued decline in the quality of public education. Not meeting state standards is gross negligence and completely unacceptable. Don't let it get any worse. I will not let this town go another year at the bottom of the totem pole. If you will elect me as your public servant, I will serve this town and the needs of its people. Those needs will change over time, but right now, as of today, the top priority is education, knowledge—the most precious and valuable resource a person can have. Vote Mahoney this Tuesday, and you'll be voting a promising new future for this town and its youngest residents.

Ex. 15-6-1: *Write a public speech asking for donation for dogs.*

Tips:

This chapter deals with different writings for delivery: reports, proposals, seminars, presentations and public speaking. No matter what forms the writings are in, the similarity of this kind of writing is that you should keep the audience/reader in consideration in the process of writing. As for the skills of delivery, it is beyond the scope of this book.

Suggested Answers

Keys to Ex. 1-2-1 (P004)

1. At the counter, we asked when the plane would arrive.
2. He got rid of all the mistakes in his notes.
3. She thought about his words carefully.
4. Paul was fired.
5. Please turn off the lights before leaving the room.
6. Unfortunately, we cannot help you.
7. Our university is close to an amusement park.
8. Terry believes that everything will be OK.

Keys to Ex. 1-3-1 (P010)

1. Come early, or you'll be late for the school.
2. It must be raining now, for everyone carries an umbrella.
3. The engineer who is talking there is Jack's father.
4. Do you believe in the saying that "Blood is thicker than water"?
5. The director, in fact, has done very little work.
6. The Temple of Heaven, he said, is like a fairyland.
7. She was born on Aug. 5, 1996.
8. "I mean... Well, I mean we needn't come back so early."
9. No one is born with knowledge; knowledge must be taught and learned.
10. Christopher G. Hayes wrote a very useful book for students: *English at Hand* (2003).
11. The drowning girl was screaming, "Help! Help!"
12. On the fourth of July, we celebrate the War of Independence; on Labor Day, we celebrate contributions of organized labor to American life.
13. As a salesperson, he lives by this motto: "Never sell a product I myself have never used and like."
14. Poor management, insufficient supplies of raw material and shortage of skilled workers—these are the main reason for the failure of this enterprise.

Keys to Ex. 1-4-1 (P016)

1. The reply is always "Not Today."

2. On Sunday, October 10, we spent the night in Oklahoma; the next day we flew to South America.

3. While waiting for the dentist, I read an article on American Politics in an old issue of *U.S. News & World Report*.

4. My dog is eight years old—that's fifty-six in people years.

5. I like the good old days when Lincoln's Birthday always fell on February 12.

6. Spelling errors involving the substitution of *d* for *t* in such words as *partner* and *pretty* reflect a tendency in pronunciation.

7. Tina now has 1,145 records in her collection.

8. I will have the first appointment with my eye doctor, Dr. C. I. Glass early next month.

9. For letter writing, you can refer to *The Random House Handbook*.

10. My courses in this semester include English Grammar, American History, General Psychology and Computer Operation.

Keys to Ex. 1-5-2-1 (P017)

1. Great happiness followed.

2. My nervousness disturbed me of my sleep.

3. The desire to love and be loved is universal.

4. My first sight at sea was disappointing.

5. The flight of stairs brings us to the top.

6. Poor health deprives people of a happy life.

7. My inability to concentrate on my studies worried me even more.

Keys to Ex. 1-6-1-1 (P021)

Word	Denotation	Connotation	Sentence
gold	symbol *Au*, a soft, yellow, corrosion-resistant element	something valuable	Silence is gold.
blood	red liquid running in the blood vessel	close relationship	Blood is thicker than water.
mother	the female parent	protectiveness, affection	Failure is the mother of success.
weed	grass in wild	uneducated person	Don't be such a weed!

Keys to Ex. 1-6-2-1 (P021)

1. little; small;   2. childlike; childish;   3. modest; humble;

4. cheap; inexpensive;   5. mean; economical.

Keys to Ex. 1-6-2-2 (P022)

family; happy; problems; proper; little; early; learned; questioned; consequences; family; elders; paid

Keys to Ex. 1-7-1 (P028)

1. More than half of the city was affected by the flood.
2. War and peace remains a constant theme in history.
3. Sufficient data have been collected.
4. The Philippines lies to the south-east of China.
5. The singer and dancer intends to attend our evening.
6. Three weeks is allowed for making the preparation.
7. There is a pen, a knife and several books on the desk.
8. The shelf full of books and magazines stands in the corner of the room.

Keys to Ex. 1-7-2 (P028)

1. On arriving at the airport, the president made a speech.
2. It is necessary to read extensively to be well-informed.
3. Astronauts must be intelligent, cool-headed and exceptionally healthy.
4. Jack decided to get a job rather than to go to the university.
5. Listening carefully to the teacher in class saves work later.
6. After the traffic accident, I opened my eyes slowly and realized I was still alive.

Keys to Ex. 1-7-3 (P028)

1. Attentive listening betrays the mistakes.
2. Her belief that the ship could be saved prompted her to call the volunteers for help.
3. It pains me to think that she has to overwork every day.
4. When the speaker was not audible, I asked him to repeat.
5. Suzhou is the home to some 2,000 pavilions and towers.
6. China's civilization ranks among the world's oldest civilizations.
7. His selflessness, diligence and honesty enabled him to become a great scientist.
8. Her long confinement to bed had impaired the function of her ankles.
9. A careful study of Mars through a telescope will reveal a number of dark, blue-green markings.

Keys to Ex. 2-2-1-1 (P032)

Some people disagree with the statement that the use of private cars should be greatly encouraged in China now, especially in big cities. Their main reasons are as follows. To begin with, too many private cars in big cities will make the present situation of traffic worse. The traffic will become even more crowded. Second, more traffic accidents will happen if many private cars run in the limited streets. Third, cars will result in air pollution, which has already been a big headache to big cities. Finally, the parking space in big cities is limited, and too many cars will need more space that some cities cannot afford now. To sum up, it is not the time to advocate the private cars in China.

Keys to Ex. 2-2-1-2 (P032)

*The Internet is very popular among the Chinese. Many people like shopping online becau*se shopping on the Internet makes our life more convenient and comfortable. We don't need to go outside and search for what we need in the shops one by one. We can even buy the goods in foreign countries through Internet. In this way, our precious time and energy is saved. Besides, items sold online are often of nicer price than those in shops. This is because there is no middle merchant between the seller and the buyer. In brief, more smart shoppers turn to Network for better bargains.

Keys to Ex. 2-2-2-1 (P033)

Drinks may be classified into two main groups: alcoholic and non-alcoholic. Alcoholic drinks refer to the beverages such as spirits, wine and beer while non-alcoholic drinks include two categories: hot and cold. The hot non-alcoholic drinks consist of tea, coffee and cocoa, and cold non-alcoholic drinks fall into two kinds: aerated and non-aerated. Drinks as lemonade, tonic water, soda water or coke all belong to the former, whereas the latter can be subdivided as the squash or cordial, the fruit juices and the other drinks as milk.

Keys to Ex. 2-2-2-2 (P033)

The universities and colleges in China can be divided in the following ways. First, they can be classified into state leading universities, provincial key universities and local colleges. The state leading universities such as Peking and Tsinghua are financed by the Education Ministry to maintain high-level research and teaching, while provincial key universities are supported by their provinces and local colleges by local governments.

The second criterion to divide them is according to academic fields. Some of them can be categorized into comprehensive universities, and some into foreign languages universities, some into universities of science and engineering. The universities and colleges can also be grouped into private and public ones. Currently, most universities are public whereas few are private.

Keys to Ex. 2-2-3-1 (P034)

6-2-4-3-5-1

Keys to Ex. 2-2-3-2 (P035)

There are several reasons for the boom in celebrating foreign festivals on Chinese campuses. In the first place, it is the product of students' seeking after individuality and novelty, for which the college campus offers an ideal climate. Furthermore, it is regarded, among the students, as a perfect means of freeing themselves from academic stress, since most college students are subject to the pressure from all sides. In conclusion, it is an inevitable result of more and more exchanges between Western and Eastern cultures.

Keys to Ex. 2-2-4-1 (P036)

on the other hand; but; while; by contrast; Although; but

Keys to Ex. 2-2-4-2 (P036)

When traveling, people like to join package tours, as this mode of traveling is said to be most convenient; others prefer individual travel for freedom. It is true that joining a package tour can bring great convenience. We do not need to worry about lodging and board, nor about the transportation. But at the sight of the guide's flag waving, we have to take ourselves away from the scenes we are marveling at and follow the guide whose sole concern is to cover all spots according to the schedule, regardless of the weather or the tourists' health condition. On the contrary, the individual travel gives more freedom. However, although it is of great essence to arrange the tour up by ourselves, it is rather troublesome to mange everything within the plan.

Keys to Ex. 2-2-5-1 (P037)

Presently, there are many means of transportation for people to travel by. One of the best, for example, would be the airplane. It is fast and rather comfortable. By taking a plane, we will save a lot of time and get something urgent done quickly.

My favorite transport means is by train. I like to take a train because I can enjoy good scenery through the windows. In addition, I can talk with other people on the train. Most trains offer good services and have sleeping couches where I can easily spend a night.

Keys to Ex. 2-2-5-2 (P037)

Decorating a dormitory room is a challenge. Last Sunday, we decided to decorate our fourteen-square-meter room for the May Day. We went shopping from store to store, and finally bought wallpaper, pictures and some plastic flowers. Then, we spent the whole day sticking the wallpaper, rearranging the furniture so that the pictures and flowers would stand out best. However, comments from girls in our class were very discouraging. They said that the room was still an absolute mess.

Key to Ex. 3-1-1 (P045)

The writer uses the third person.

Keys to Ex. 3-2-1 (P046)

"*The Road to Adulthood*" is an excellent narrative because it has something unique to say. The writer's purpose is to show us the difficulty and hardship toward the process of youth growth—a harmonization of the individual's mind and heart and in a unification of selfhood and identity within the broader society. The thesis could be spotted in the beginning paragraph: "*I was positive that blond waves were just what I needed to acquire the maturity of popularity so essential in the third grade.*" and the last paragraph: "*In a way I feel that such a fruitless journey to the hairdresser actually helped me a bit further along the road to adulthood, since it was a perfect example of a disappointing obstacle that can be improved only by time and patience, and not by tantrums.*"

Keys to Ex. 3-3-1 (P047)

1. The purpose is to show the absurdity of "fishing enforcement" made by the police officer in Los Angeles.

2. ① The who—Ralph and Ilene, the undercover police officer. ② The where—Los Angeles. ③ The when—Baseball Game Day.

3. ① The beginning: Ralph and Ilene planned to be out to a baseball game. ② The middle: The traffic was lighter than they expected. They arrived at the stadium before game time and decided to buy tickets from a scalper. ③ The end: Ralph was handcuffed, for the local government wants to enforce all the laws that bring in money.

4. The narrative is written in chronological order. First, the story teller introduces the total time needed to watch the ball game—travelling time is longer than the game time. Next, they spent an hour to prepare the trip, and then it took them 40 minutes to get to the stadium. Finally, they had to spend about 20 minutes in argument with the undercover police officer.

Keys to Ex. 3-4-1 (P048)

1. The writer's purpose is to show us the danger of overuse of computers in the information age. His main ideas may be summed up as follows: though there may be great advantages in using the computer in schools, it should not be made to replace a human teacher; while individual coaching in education is good, peer help should also be encouraged; and educators should not overlook children's enjoyment of acquiring knowledge with their friends.

2. Yes. They are made quite clear.

　　The who—Maggie and Tommy

　　The where—"School"

The when—May 17, 2155

3. The body is made up of relevant and interesting details. The description often goes hand in hand with narration, for the writer needs to describe the old book, the mechanical teacher, the County Inspector and Margie's schoolroom when he tells his story. They are well chosen, for they help to bring out the main idea of the narrative. The end is short and forceful. It points out the significance of the narrative with the last words echoing the topic "The Fun They Had."

Keys to Ex. 4-1 (P053)

I feel the <u>delicate</u> symmetry of a leaf. I pass my hands lovingly about the <u>smooth</u> skin of a silver birch, or the <u>rough</u> bark of a pine. In spring I touch the branches of trees <u>hopefully</u> in search of a bud, the first sign of <u>awakening</u> Nature after her winter's sleep. I feel the <u>delightful</u> texture of a flower, and discover its <u>remarkable</u> folds; and something of the miracle of Nature is revealed to me. <u>Occasionally,</u> if I am very fortunate, I place my hand <u>gently</u> in a small tree and feel the <u>happy</u> quiver of a bird in full song. I am delighted to have <u>cool</u> water of a brook rush through my <u>open</u> fingers. To me, a <u>thick</u> carpet of pine needles or <u>soft</u> grass is more welcome than the most <u>luxurious</u> Persian rug. To me, the <u>colorful</u> seasons are a <u>thrilling</u> and <u>unending</u> drama, the action of which streams through my finger tips.

I <u>feel</u> the delicate symmetry of a leaf. I <u>pass</u> my hands lovingly about the smooth skin of a silver birch, or the rough bark of a pine. In spring I <u>touch</u> the branches of trees hopefully in search of a bud, the first sign of awakening Nature after her winter's sleep. I <u>feel</u> the delightful texture of a flower, and <u>discover</u> its remarkable folds; and something of the miracle of Nature is revealed to me. Occasionally, if I am very fortunate, I <u>place my hand</u> gently in a small tree and feel the happy quiver of a bird in full song. I am delighted to <u>have cool water of a brook rush through</u> my open fingers. To me, a thick carpet of pine needles or soft grass is more welcome than the most luxurious Persian rug. To me, the colorful seasons are a thrilling and unending drama, the action of which <u>streams through</u> my finger tips.

Keys to Ex. 4-2 (P053)

1. This description takes spatial order to describe the campus.

2. All the objects are described according to a central focus: The beautiful campus plays an important part in students' life.

3. An elegant pavilion, white stone benches, the woods with all kinds of trees, a flower bed with hundreds of flowers in full bloom, lawns on both sides of the gate, carps.

4. Color, sound and smell.

5. Beautiful, elegant, fantastic, gently, intoxicating, leisurely.

6. Personification. "An elegant pavilion standing right in the center." "You can listen to the birds

singing in the woods and the trees talking with the wind gently."

Keys to Ex. 4-3 (P054)

1. This description takes spatial order to describe the study, which is from left to right, top to bottom, far to near.

2. All the objects are described according to a central focus: how it is used and what part it plays in helping building characters of the writer.

3. Details are: the Guatemalan crucifix, the window, the old-fashioned doctor's desk, the computer, his dog Chico, book cases, the watercolor on the wall, the seat, the coffee, the cup and the tray.

4. Size, shape, color, texture, and smell.

5. Cozy, big cheerful window, freshly perked coffee, etc.

6. Personification. A lot of things that are not human are given human-like qualities. Examples are: "Birds chirp outside, beckoning you to enter." "When I turn him on, he'll crackle 'hello' and blink an inviting amber command on the screen." "A bronzed Indian chief in a watercolor squints knowingly at us from the wall."

Key to Ex. 15-2-1 (P181)

Dear Mr. Keating,

In response to your enquiry about Sungreen Power, the company seems to be performing well.

One thing to consider is their new sales agreement with Mainline Energy, worth 190 million Euros. This should help their share price which recently halved. On the one hand, this was caused by a shortage of silicon, but on the other hand, Sungreen specializes in technology which requires less silicon.

So despite the fall, I would still suggest you consider investing. The fact that solar power costs have continuously fallen since the early nineties and look set to equal Norman energy costs in the next few years makes this a good investment opportunity.

Feel free to call me to discuss any further queries you might have.

Best wishes,
Tony Brown

Key to Ex. 15-6-1 (P186)

You know those friends who are perpetually there for you? Whether you need a ride home at 2 in the morning or you're sick and they come bring you soup, you just know you can always count on them to have your back. Well, that's sort of like the friendship a dog brings to your life.

It doesn't matter if you've been gone from the house for four minutes or four hours, dogs are always ecstatic to see you again. You could throw a stick across the lawn all afternoon and they'll act like their brilliant master has created the best, most exciting game on the planet. They can sense when you are ill and lie protectively near you. They can sense when you are sad and lick your hand affectionately. They are extraordinarily affectionate and intuitive creatures. However, not all of them are lucky enough to have an owner whom they can love and adore.

Twice a week, we welcome a new addition to our family at Cute "N" Cuddly Canines, which means we house just over a hundred dogs in this shelter every year. We love all of the animals who come to us for as long as they were meant to be on this Earth, so, as you can imagine, it's getting a bit crowded, and resources are slight.

This is why we are currently seeking donations for our little shelter, which has been here in town for the last 75 years. We do not turn dogs away, nor do we euthanize them; therefore, we need to expand to accommodate this growing family of man's best friends.

We survive thanks to the help of our dedicated volunteers, but the water and electricity are not free—nor are the leashes, shampoo, flea dip, collars, toys, bedding, cleaning supplies, cages, food, towels, toothbrushes, slings, mail trimmers, medication, harnesses, and everything else that keeps this shelter running.

Many of our volunteers spend up to eight hours a day at the shelter, making sure that each of our fury friends feels comfortable and loved. There is only so much these people can do. However, with their limited resources, some of the ladies have even taken to purchasing dog food on their own dimes to make sure no one has to go hungry.

We are asking for a little help for the town's most vulnerable inhabitants. The smallest of donations makes a world of difference and we are eternally grateful for the support we have gotten over the years.

Aside from the official donation page, we are also having a very special event on May 20 to which you are cordially invited. From 8 am at the community center, there will be a wonderful day of festivities, and every cent of the proceeds will go toward the shelter. We hope to see everyone there. From the giant Mastiffs to the teacup Yorkies, the doggies thank you, the staff thank you and I thank you for your time and compassion.

And, of course, if your family is looking for a cuddy canine to call your very own, you know where to look. We have adoption fairs every Saturday at the shelter, and we hope to get every single puppy a loving and caring home.